Variety in Contemporary English

Second Edition

TITLES OF RELATED INTEREST

English Word Stress
Erik Fudge

Essentials of English Grammar
Otto Jespersen

Introducing English Grammar
David J. Young

Language and Literature
edited by Ronald Carter

Language, Discourse and Literature
edited by Ronald Carter and Paul Simpson

On The Surface of Discourse
Michael Hoey

Syntax (Second Edition)
Keith Brown and Jim Miller

Towards a Contextual Grammar of English
Eugene Winter

Vocabulary
Ronald Carter

Variety in Contemporary English

Second Edition

W. R. O'DONNELL
and
LORETO TODD

HarperCollins *Academic*
An imprint of HarperCollins *Publishers*

Published by
HarperCollins*Academic*
77–85 Fulham Palace Road
Hammersmith
London W6 8JB
UK

10 East 53rd Street
New York, NY 10022
USA

First published in 1980 by Unwin Hyman Ltd.
Second edition 1991

British Library Cataloguing in Publication Data

O'Donnell, W. R. (William Robert) *1925–*
    Variety in contemporary English. – 2nd ed.
    1. English language
    I. Title   II. Todd, Loreto
    420

    ISBN 0-04-445737-5

Library of Congress Cataloging in Publication Data

A catalog record for this book is
available from the Library of Congress.

Typeset in 9 on 11 point Times by Fotographics (Bedford) Ltd
and printed in Great Britain by
Billing and Sons Ltd, London and Worcester

Contents

Preface

This book is intended as an introduction to the study of English language. It is aimed primarily at college and university students, particularly those who are likely in due course to find themselves teaching a language, whether English or some other, but it is hoped that it may prove interesting and instructive to others; to practising teachers, to sixth form pupils and to the intelligent layman.

It is not a book about linguistics. As a discipline, linguistics has flourished in recent years, multiplying theories beyond the capacity of any single mind to comprehend, but in doing so it has, in our view, tended to lose touch with the realities of normal human language. The search for elegant answers has, paradoxically, obscured an important aspect of the original problem; the multi-dimensional diversity of language in use. In this book we have tried to describe that diversity, and though we have done so exclusively in terms of English we believe that budding linguists might do well to start here, with the raw material of linguistics, rather than with abstract theory.

We are aware that our account is not exhaustive even for English: each chapter could with ease have been expanded into a sizeable volume. But, as we have said above, we intend this book as an introduction. That is why every chapter concludes with a list of works for 'additional reading'. Our view of education is that knowledge is not something to be handed on piece by piece from person to person, but rather that each individual has to work to construct his own knowledge out of his reading and experience. We have addressed ourselves accordingly to the reader's understanding and not to his memory, and the additional reading is suggested in order that he may develop and extend his understanding beyond our introductory account.

We have ourselves made extensive use of the works listed. Where we have been conscious of a specific debt we have acknowledged it in the text, but we should also like to acknowledge a more general debt to these works and their authors. We have not, of course, confined ourselves to published sources and most of our examples are therefore drawn from personal experience and study.

Apart from the help we have received from the writings of others we should also like to acknowledge how much we owe to past discussions with our teachers, our colleagues and our students. And we should like to record our particular gratitude to Professor Angus McIntosh of the University of Edinburgh, who read and commented on an early draft of this book. We hope we have made full use of his valuable advice. The imperfections that remain, of course, are entirely our responsibility.

Finally, we should like to thank Mrs Joan Colman and Miss Jenny Wilcock for their kind help with the typing.

Leeds, September 1979

Acknowledgements

The authors and publishers wish to thank the following who have kindly given permission for the use of copyright material: Stephen Leslie for extracts from 'Seven Bloody Years' and 'Thoughts'; and Sangster's Book Stores Ltd., Kingston, Jamaica, for an extract from Louise Bennett's poem 'No Little Twang'.

Conventions

We have kept our use of symbols and conventions to a minimum but the following summary may prove useful.

* An asterisk indicates that the structure following is unacceptable. Italics are used to indicate emphasis.

‘ ’ Single quotation marks are used to indicate quotations. They are also used to draw attention to important terms as they are introduced in the text.

< > Such brackets indicate graphemes, i.e. they indicate written rather than spoken segments.

/ / Slants enclose a phonemic transcription. The consonantal values of English are applicable to the consonants enclosed in slants but we should like to emphasise that /s/ always has the value of ‘s’ in ‘sing’ and never of ‘s’ in ‘goes’. Three additional vocalic symbols are used:

/ɪ/ has the value of ‘i’ in such words as ‘bit’, ‘fit’ or ‘did’

/ɛ/ has the value of ‘e’ in such words as ‘bet’, ‘get’ or ‘peck’

/o/ has the value of ‘o’ in such words as ‘got’, ‘not’ or ‘knock’.

˘ is placed over a syllable to indicate that it is unstressed.

/ is placed over a syllable to indicate that it is stressed.

Ø represents ‘zero’. + Ø means that nothing is added to the preceding word.

ME Middle English, a composite term for the varieties of English spoken between 1100 and 1500.

OE Old English, a composite term for the varieties of English spoken before 1100.

ON Old Norse, a composite term for the Viking dialects spoken before 1100.

RP Received Pronunciation, a term applied to an English class accent originally associated with public schools and the older universities and now also associated with BBC English.

1 Speech and Writing

In the modern world, with its networks of communication, it is very unlikely that there remains a single community that has somehow or other managed to escape 'discovery'. But if such a community does exist, there is one thing about it of which we can be entirely certain: its members are able to communicate very complex messages to one another by means of speech. So fundamental is this ability to human society that we should find it difficult to imagine a community of truly human beings which lacked it.

On the other hand, it would surprise nobody to discover that communication by writing was unknown to our hypothetical community. It remained unknown to many flourishing human societies in the past, indeed to most of them, and it continues to be unknown to very large numbers of people even today.

But, of course, there are many societies which do possess this additional mode of communication. These tend to be the technologically advanced communities. Just as speech is a defining characteristic of 'humanness', so may writing be regarded as a defining characteristic of technological advancement. This is mainly because the relative permanence of writing makes it possible to overcome limitations of time and space in passing on useful knowledge from person to person.

Evidently, English-speaking communities are among those which have access to both means of communication: both speech and writing. And so, before we go on to discuss other kinds of variety, we propose to take a look at how English varies between these two modes. We hope in doing so to illuminate not only the relationship of the two to one another, but also that between them both and language.

Having both means of communication available is not a simple matter of having an alternative. Indeed, it is not in any sense at all a simple matter. However, we can make it easier to understand if we consider the relationship between speech and writing from a number of different, but related, points of view. Accordingly our discussion will be divided into four sections:

Substance
Operation

Use
Acquisition

In order to understand what is implied here by the term 'substance', it is necessary to perceive that speech and writing are not themselves language, but rather vehicles, or *mediums*, for language.

The distinction is probably in need of some elaboration. It is not the kind of distinction which may be verified directly by the senses, but rather one that has to be constructed by the mind and one which, accordingly, needs careful thought before it is properly understood. There are, of course, many distinctions which can be verified directly by the senses: cats and dogs; rough and smooth; chalk and cheese. Our intellects are barely engaged in perceiving such distinctions, because both the elements distinguished exist in the concrete, observable world. The difficulty about distinguishing language from medium arises because only one of the elements, medium, exists in that world. The other element, language, belongs in the abstract, theoretical world, which is impossible to observe directly.

A helpful analogy is available in the distinction between money on the one hand, and the monetary system on the other. By money is meant the pieces of metal and paper we carry around with us in order to be able to buy the things we want. Clearly money is concrete and observable. However, the values attributed to individual coins and banknotes are not related to their *intrinsic* worth. There is no real sense, for instance, in which one hundred of the pieces of metal we call 'pence' are worth one of the pieces we call 'pound'. The values of these things are, rather, *extrinsic*; that is to say, these values are conferred from outside, in fact by the community. But these values are not conferred at random. They are conferred by reference to an abstract system of values in terms of which their relationship to one another is defined. This abstract system is the monetary system, and coins and banknotes are thus merely tokens representing particular points in the monetary system. Coins and banknotes may be changed by the community so far as their size, shape and composition are concerned, with relatively little inconvenience; as indeed happens from time to time. But any change in the abstract system in terms of which we assign values to the individual tokens causes great upheaval, and may take several years to accomplish.

The alternative to having money linked to an abstract system of (monetary) values is to have a barter system, which operates on the basis of intrinsic values; so many goats for so much flour, for example. But language does not function in this way. The noises we make and the marks we inscribe have, generally speaking, no intrinsic language value, but function rather in the manner of coins and banknotes; as tokens, carriers of a value conferred upon them by reference to the abstract language system. Our speech and our writing mean nothing of themselves. They only mean something if we can relate them to the language system. Thus, when you hear spoken a language you do not know, you can perceive the medium, may even be able to recognise and repeat correctly some recurring patterns of sound, but you are not able to attach any meaning to the sounds because you cannot relate them to the appropriate abstract system in terms of which alone those noises make sense, have meaning, to the people who make them.

The distinction the reader is being asked to perceive is represented, somewhat simplistically, in Figure 1.

Figure 1

ABSTRACT	CONCRETE
Language	Medium
(e.g. English)	(speech, writing . . .)

Perhaps we can make this figure clearer by means of a particular instance. Thus, in English and many other languages a distinction is made between 'singular' and 'plural'. Ignoring the few exceptional cases, the tokens by which this abstract distinction is made concrete in English are as follows:

(a)   speech

singular: Ø ; e.g. cat, dog, horse
plural: /s/, e.g. in cats
or /z/, e.g. in dogs
or /ɪz/), e.g. in horses.

That is, the base form without addition is assigned the value singular, and the base form with the addition of sounds /s/ or /z/ or /ɪz/ (depending on the phonetic context) has the value plural.

(b)   writing

singular: Ø
plural: (-s); e.g. in cats, dogs and horses
(-es); e.g. in matches

Such distinctions may be set out as in Figure 2. (It should be noted in passing that codes such as Morse Code and drum 'language' are parasitic, in that they cannot be interpreted unless they are first related to the appropriate medium; writing in the case of Morse, and speech in the case of drums. However, 'signing' among deaf people, as distinct from simple finger spelling, should probably be regarded as a different medium.)

It is important to observe, with reference to Figure 2, that in understanding the singular/plural distinction it is not necessary either to say aloud what has been written down, or to write down what has been said aloud. It is possible to perceive a singular or a plural ending in either medium, without any reference whatsoever to the other.

Figure 2

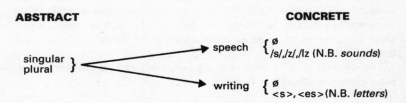

However, the main point of Figure 2 is this: many languages, though not all, distinguish singular from plural, but no two languages signal that distinction in exactly the same way. On the other hand, most languages will make some use of the sound /s/, let us say, but there will be no other language in which it performs exactly the function it does in English with regard to signifying plural.

In terms of this figure it should be clear that knowing English is not just a matter of being able to detect and reproduce significant differences of sound, any more than it is only a matter of understanding such a distinction as that between singular and plural. Rather, knowing English, or knowing any language, consists in being able to relate the two: to understand, that is, just which distinctions in sound (or in writing) correspond to which abstract distinctions in the mind.

Moreover, since either medium may, as we noted above, function independently of the other, it should be equally clear that it is erroneous to regard writing as just a means of recording speech. Instead, we must regard the two as different substances having concrete existence in the real world, and able to take varying shapes, as it were, and signify abstract distinctions in the mind. In a word, the two are 'mediums', just as metal and paper are mediums for an abstract monetary system, except, of course, that language systems are much more complex.

It has to be admitted that many very eminent linguists, including Leonard Bloomfield, the most influential linguist of his day, have taken a different view of the relationship between speech and writing from the one explained above. It is generally argued by such scholars that writing is a relatively recent development in mankind's linguistic behaviour – with many languages existing only in spoken form even today – and consequently that writing is only a secondary medium, parasitic on speech, the latter alone being the true object of the linguist's study. Some have gone so far as virtually to identify language with speech; the following quotation is fairly representative: '. . . a language is a system of arbitrary vocal symbols by means of which a social group co-operates' (Bloch and Trager, p. 5). However, the position we have adopted and attempted to explain is probably the more widely-held view at the present time, and seems to us the more reasonable.

The substances of the two mediums differ from one another in every important particular. The substance of speech is sound. When you speak, what you actually do is expel air, just as you do when breathing out, except that you disturb and modify the air at various points in its journey from the lungs to the outside atmosphere. These disturbances can be detected by the eardrums of everyone within 'earshot'. The disturbances follow one another – fairly rapidly – in time, requiring little effort or preparation to produce and needing no extra equipment or tool; we simply adapt certain body organs for the purpose. However, this substance suffers from two important disadvantages; (a) it does not last, and (b) it is effective only over relatively short distances.

The possibilities offered by such devices as the telephone and the tape-recorder modify the validity of this last statement to some extent. Nowadays, after all, it is possible to carry such devices around with you and speak to someone on the other side of the world almost as easily as you can to someone standing by your side, or record important conversations and memoranda at will. Nevertheless, the statement is still true in general. These devices are really relatively rare and their use exceptional. They are remote from the experience of most of humanity, and were entirely absent from our history. Characteristically, therefore, speech is subject to the limitations we have specified.

By contrast, think of what you do when you write. First, you have to hold a tool of some kind in your hand, or perhaps tap on a machine, in order to produce marks on a contrasting background. These are perceived by the eye, not by the ear; and so quite distinct senses are involved. Furthermore, the substance of writing is organised in space; not in time. It is also produced somewhat more laboriously than speech, but on the other hand, once produced it is relatively permanent and easy to transport, and so writing may be effective over great distances of space and time. These differences between the two substances are summed up for convenience in Figure 3.

Figure 3

		SPEECH	WRITING
substance	:	disturbance of the air	marks on e.g. paper
produced by	:	lungs and 'vocal organs'	hands
perceived by	:	ear	eye
organised in	:	time	space
production	:	quick, easy	(relatively) slow, laborious
tools?	:	no*	yes
permanent?	:	no*	yes
transportable?	:	no*	yes

* Excluding tape-recorders and such.

From the point of view of their respective substances, therefore, speech and writing differ totally. It follows that there can be no *necessary* relationship between the two mediums, and, as we have already remarked, either medium may function in complete independence of the other, so that we do not need to read something aloud in order to understand it, or alternatively, write something down in order to understand it.

And yet, as we all know, it is possible to write down what is said, or say what is written down, if desired. For instance, lecturers preparing lectures will often write down what they later propose to say aloud and, by the same token, their students may write down at least some of what they hear. Though there is no *necessary* relationship between the two totally different substances of speech and writing, therefore, there must clearly be some conventional link between the two to make it possible to transpose from one to the other.

It is important to appreciate that this link is in principle distinct from the conventional links we have seen to exist between each of the mediums, on the one hand, and the language system, on the other. In other words, the ability to say aloud what has been written down, and write down what has been said is not dependent upon understanding. For instance, the reader should have no difficulty in speaking aloud the following passage correctly at first sight, though it is unlikely that many readers will understand it completely at a first reading.

> Since the elements in a field are always subordinated to the whole, every local modification engendering a refashioning of the ensemble, the first law of perceptual totalities is that the whole, over and beyond its having quantitative features of its own, has a quantitative value different from the sum of its parts. (J. Piaget, *Structuralism*, Routledge & Kegan Paul, 1971)

It follows, then, that the conventional link must be a direct one between the two substances, one in which units of some kind perceived in one substance relate to units of a different kind in an entirely dissimilar substance. In other words, what we have is a position such as that shown in Figure 4.

Figure 4

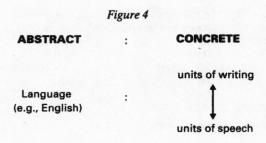

ABSTRACT   :   **CONCRETE**

Language   :
(e.g., English)

The origin of the link between the two substances lies in the fact that speech developed first in human society, and for a very long time was the only medium. Accordingly, when writing proper eventually did begin to develop it was possible, and clearly in many ways advantageous, to identify units of the writing system with units derived from an analysis, however impressionistic, of the spoken language. Thus it is that all contemporary writing systems, though they differ radically from one another in many respects, at least agree in being based upon symbols which correspond to units perceived in the spoken language.

The units of the spoken language to which the written symbols correspond need not be units of sound. Traditional Chinese writing, for instance, is based upon characters which correspond to units of meaning, and the same characters may be pronounced quite differently in different dialects of Chinese. Such a system is not so remote from our own experience as we may suppose. Thus, any literate European would understand the character '2', let us say, but speakers of different languages would pronounce it quite differently from one another.

However, apart from a few odd symbols, e.g. £, +, =, 2, 3, etc., the English writing system is not of this type. It is what is called an 'alphabetic' system. That is to say, the writing system of English is based upon an inventory of symbols, called 'letters', which correspond, though very roughly, to units perceived in the stream of sound. These sound units are not actual segments of speech, but rather idealisations of actual segments. They are called 'phonemes'. A writing system which provided for a one-to-one correspondence between letters and phonemes would be a 'phonemic' alphabet. No actual language possesses such an alphabet, though some of them, for example, Spanish and Polish, come a good deal closer to it than does English. In English, as is well known, the correspondences between letters of the alphabet and phonemes is irregular and inconsistent, so that foreigners frequently complain about English spelling and even educated native speakers can make mistakes.

Fortunately, the lack of regular and consistent correspondences is not so big a disadvantage as is popularly supposed. It does mean that English spelling is more difficult to learn than is the case with some other languages, but it does not really lead to any difficulties in reading, because we do not read letter by letter, even when we are reading aloud. On the other hand, though actual reading is not made difficult, *learning* to read may be, for reasons which will become apparent later, when we discuss acquisition (and see Chapter 8).

The natural differences which we recognise in the substances of speech and writing lead to differences in the way the two mediums operate.

Thus, the ease and rapidity of production of speech means it is the medium best suited to addressing someone present, in response to some immediate motive. However, this in turn means that little time can be given to planning or revision, and so speech in operation is characteristically broken up by 'fillers' of various sorts; for example, 'I mean', 'sort of', 'you know', 'you see'. It is also sometimes marked by syntactic incompleteness, by breaks and hesitations, and by a good deal of repetition.

All these features may be attributed to the spontaneous nature of speech. The presence of the addressee, however, does mean that the communication is helped by non-linguistic, but linguistically significant, phenomena, such as gesture, posture and facial expression (see Chapter 4). Things apparent in the shared situation may not need to be spelt out; so that reference to a person in full view of both speaker and addressee may be accomplished by means of a personal pronoun, where writing might call for a full description. Furthermore, the act of communication may be helped by the addressee; for example, by questions, a puzzled expression, encouraging noises or nods, which let the speaker know whether he is being understood or whether there is something he should repeat or explain.

Writing contrasts in every possible respect. First of all, it normally has an absent addressee, and is not well adapted, in any case, to satisfying immediate needs. This means that writing calls for an ability to think ahead and plan. But, by the same token, time is usually available for redrafting and revision. Good writing, in fact, demands very careful planning, and it is quite mistaken to believe that spontaneity is a source of excellence in writing, though sometimes, in certain uses, writing may achieve its object by *appearing* spontaneous. But, characteristically, because of planning and redrafting, writing is relatively smoother syntactically and in every other way: no fillers, no incomplete constructions and no hesitations (except when such features are deliberately introduced for some special effect).

The absence of the addressee means that the writer is not helped by such paralinguistic devices as gestures, facial expression and posture. Nor can there be any immediate response from the addressee to tell the writer how effective he is being. And, finally, so far as the shared situation is concerned, there is little to be taken for granted beyond those few assumptions that go with a shared language. If understanding is to be ensured, therefore, the writer must be much more explicit than the speaker needs to be: another reason for careful planning and revising.

However, because writing is relatively permanent, and organised in space rather than in time, it is possible to have long stretches in front of you to study and ponder over, and so we are able to understand sentences and paragraphs which would present problems in speech. Certainly it is nowadays possible to record speech, and in this way we can make it relatively permanent, so that we may have sentences and paragraphs played over as often as necessary for understanding. But speech, even so, remains organised in time, and this, for some reason, is not nearly so convenient and helpful for the human mind. If this point is not already clear the reader should try recording a complex paragraph both on tape and in writing and see which is easier to deal with from the point of view of understanding. It may, of course, be that the difference is merely a product of our literary type of education.

Differences in the natural properties of the two mediums, and differences in the way they operate, lead in turn to differences in the uses to which they are put.

As we noted at the beginning, speech developed first, and even today there are many spoken languages which have no written counterpart. This raises two rather interesting points:

(1) If speech met all communication needs there is no reason why writing should ever have developed at all.
(2) It is the less technologically advanced societies which lack a writing system.

Taking these two considerations together suggests that once a human society reaches a certain stage of development new language needs begin to arise, needs we should surely be justified in regarding as more sophisticated. And continued development beyond this stage seems to demand the introduction of a new medium adapted to these needs.

It is not being suggested here that the relationship between writing and the general development of a given society is a simple one. It is not the case, for instance, that the mere provision of a writing system would, by itself, ensure further development. But it does make development possible, and it is beyond dispute that all surviving advanced societies have acquired, and continue to make considerable use of, a writing system.

If we look at human societies in terms of their development over time, then, we see that speech and writing complement one another in making development possible, those communication needs which cannot be satisfied by speech being taken over by the new medium: writing.

Furthermore, if we examine an advanced society such as our own and consider the uses made of the two mediums at the present time, we shall discover that they complement one another there, too. Live speech continues to support those communication needs for which it was always most convenient, while writing must continue to respond to those needs which compelled its introduction in the first place.

The uses for which speech is most convenient tend, naturally, to be the most basic everyday uses. Its ease and rapidity of production and the possibility of augmenting it by gesture and posture make it ideal for those situations in which people come face to face, or where quickness of address and response are called for: the response, of course, not necessarily being a language response.

We may easily think of many such situations, such as greetings, buying a packet of cigarettes, consulting a doctor, telling jokes, or asking the way. Modern devices such as the telephone and tape-recorder extend the range of our voices without, on the whole, fundamentally changing the range of situations for which we use our voices. For instance, we may telephone our dentist for an appointment instead of going round to make an appointment face to face. One could always write, of course, but we do not usually do so in such a case. And, strangely enough, despite easy access to recording and broadcasting devices, more books are read now than ever before.

Certain communications are mixed. For instance, public speeches are usually written to be spoken. Sometimes, in fact, a written version is released to the press before the actual speech itself is given. Many public speakers treat their lectures as live speech situations, not realising that lectures require the kind of preparation and care that goes with good writing. They believe, usually mistakenly, that all they have to do in order to interest and inform is stand up and chat. Readers will no doubt, ruefully, recognise the type.

As well as being primary from the historical point of view, both in the species and in the individual, speech is also primary from a quantitative point of view; we all speak a great deal more than we write. It by no means follows, however, that speech is *qualitatively* primary. Indeed, it would not be difficult to make out a rather attractive case for writing in this respect.

First, as has already been pointed out, a high level of technological advancement is always associated with possession of a writing system. Moreover, once a writing system has been adopted, speech continues in use for basic, mundane needs, whereas writing is associated with more sophisticated needs, such as, for instance, study.

Again, while speech is more effective in rapid and easy communication with people who are present, it is writing which makes possible effective communication over time and space. It is writing which permits us to build upon the knowledge acquired in the past, so that it is unnecessary to rediscover everything anew with every generation. Clearly, as long as a society is restricted to speech it is severely limited with regard to the amount of knowledge that can be handed on from adult to child. Non-literate societies develop devices to extend the possibilities; for example, myth is such a device. But even so the restriction is very inhibiting to the passing on of accurate knowledge. And, apart from the handing on of useful knowledge from generation to generation, it is writing which makes it possible to disseminate knowledge throughout the world: philosophical, religious, scientific and political knowledge. The ability to read and write, in fact, is probably the most important single influence in our entire history.

Then, too, because of its more or less permanent character, writing is habitually used for purposes of official notices and records, such as for contracts, wills and insurance policies. These are not, perhaps, aesthetically pleasing uses, but they are absolutely essential to the effective functioning of a complex, advanced society.

To all of this may be added the probability that, properly used, writing is a means of learning. The necessity to do without direct response from the addressee, without gesture or visual reinforcement, compels the writer to get the message absolutely clear. The careful planning and revision that this entails clarifies and structures things we may think we know, until we come to write. Knowledge which remains incommunicable is mere private intuition and is really of very little value. The necessity to clarify our ideas for others, however, modifies our vague knowledge in a qualitative way. Once we have struggled with the act of written composition – correcting, revising, restructuring, explaining – we really understand the subject. Students frequently underestimate the importance of this property of writing and assume that they understand a topic, only to find when confronted with an examination paper that their knowledge is vague and formless and it is too late at that point to go through the structuring process properly.

If we take everything into consideration, then, we can see that there is a good case for saying that though speech is quantitatively primary, it is writing which is qualitatively the more important. Yet it is better to avoid such a conclusion, since it implies that there is, in some sense, a competition between the two mediums. This is not so. Speech and writing complement one another, and both are certainly necessary in an advanced society.

From the point of view of their acquisition there are, once again, very important differences between speech and writing.

Speech comes first in the individual as in the species. It is acquired early and unconsciously, partly because there is immediate motivation (i.e. the satisfaction of present needs), but partly also because the equipment required for speech is provided by nature. Possibly there is more teaching going on with young children than we realise, at least of an informal kind, but by and large the acquisition of speech is relatively painless for normal human beings brought up normally. Most of us remember very little of the process and cannot recall a time when we were unable to talk.

But it does not follow from this that the process of acquisition is completed in infancy. It is probably the case that most educated people have acquired some of their speech through writing. Many of us would not speak as we do had we never learned to read and write. In particular, when educated people speak Standard English they are speaking a variety of English which originated and was propagated very largely in writing. However, though many people can remember improving their fluency, and the ability to make their speech appropriate to a variety of situations, it remains true that very few are able to recall a time when they were unable to communicate freely by way of this medium.

This is not so with writing, for unlike the acquisition of speech the acquisition of writing demands a relatively high level of abstraction, which depends upon maturation, and so comes later. Writing is to speech rather as algebra is to arithmetic, requiring the same kind of intellectual sophistication.

Moreover, the learning of writing is not as well motivated as is the learning of speech. It is quite unsuited to the satisfaction of immediate needs. It demands an ability to plan ahead and defer satisfactions, and these are, again, functions of a more mature mind. It should be admitted that all learning is a complex process in which maturation and teaching play a part, so that it becomes difficult if not impossible, to disentangle the contribution of each. Some research evidence does suggest that after a certain age children can be taught to plan ahead if they are taught the language to support such planning, but on the whole experiments with language-enrichment programmes have not really been a great success, and it is clear, in any case, that before the appropriate stage of maturity children are not interested in deferred satisfactions and so have little motivation to plan ahead or learn the language of planning.

It might be pointed out, too, that writing differs from speech in requiring tools not provided by nature, so that it may be regarded as considerably less 'natural' than speech. This is another reason why writing must come later.

However, because it does come later, and because there is, as we saw earlier, a conventional link between the two mediums which makes it possible to transpose from one to the other, the writing system is normally acquired in the first instance through the spoken medium. This is why we remarked earlier that though the complexity of the link between speech and writing in English did not really make reading more difficult it probably made *learning* to read more difficult. Even so, it is evidently simpler to direct methods of teaching reading towards acquisition of the system of transposition between mediums, in the first instance.

There are, of course, several different methods available. Thus, with an alphabetic language like English, it is possible to base the teaching method on the correspondence between the written symbols, the 'letters', and the sound segments they may be said to 'stand for'. This kind of method is called a 'phonic' method.

A variant of this method is one which uses a specially designed teaching alphabet as a kind of stepping-stone to the real alphabet. The supporters of this method argue that the correspondences between letter and sound in English are so confusing and inconsistent that they present the learner with enormous problems, with which many learners never quite manage to cope. Accordingly, they use a modified alphabet which makes possible a high level of consistency in order to simplify the learning task. This modified alphabet is sufficiently like the real alphabet to facilitate the transfer of reading and writing skills to that alphabet, once these skills have been acquired with the easier one. Learners using this method, therefore, learn the standard writing system in two easier stages instead of having to master it in one difficult jump, as it were.

An entirely different method is based on word recognition rather than letter recognition, so that the child learns to say whole words rather than trying to string segments together to make words.

All the different methods have their supporters, and sometimes great controversy rages between them. However, it seems that no one method is universally effective, and a judicious mixture of methods, and a flexibility in their use, seems to work best.

No matter how effective the method, it should not be forgotten that what is being taught is only the ability to transpose from one medium to the other. The reader will no doubt recall that this ability is in principle separate from understanding. The reasoning implied by these methods is that if one can teach the child how to relate written marks to the speech system he has already acquired, the child will be able to complete the process and relate the sounds to the language system. In other words, the process hoped for is that shown in Figure 5.

Figure 5

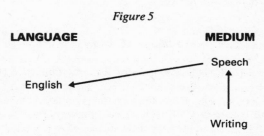

It should be borne in mind, therefore, that for the truly literate the two mediums must be capable of functioning independently, so that reading may do without the intermediacy of speech. For one thing, unless we free the reading process from its association with speech, reading is reduced to a laborious and slow exercise, held down to the speed of speech. Moreover, as the reader may easily verify for himself, it is actually more difficult to understand what is read aloud. Many teachers, for example, are familiar with the phenomenon of a pupil reading a passage out loud flawlessly without understanding a single word. The process to be aimed at for the medium of writing, therefore, is really that shown in Figure 6.

Figure 6

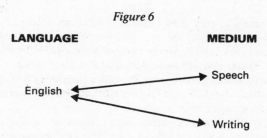

At the same time the possibility of transposition between mediums must also be retained.

Unfortunately, much less attention is usually given to this subsequent stage of acquisition of writing, in which we move from dependence on the speech link to independence of function, so that many never really acquire the ability to read properly, almost because of the early methods rather than despite them.

In this chapter we have been looking at the nature of speech and writing. We first of all distinguished them as mediums from the language to which they give substance, then we considered the fundamental differences between them, in terms of their substance, their operation, the uses to which each is put and their acquisition. We shall go on now to look closely at other kinds of difference to be found in English, beginning in the next chapter with dialect differences.

Additional Reading

Abercrombie, D. (1968), *Elements of General Phonetics* (Edinburgh: Edinburgh University Press).

Aitchison, J. (1976), *The Articulate Mammal* (London: Hutchinson).

Bloch, B. and Trager, G. (1942), *Outline of Linguistic Analysis* (Baltimore: Special Publications of the Linguistic Society of America).

Bloomfield, L. (1933), *Language* (London: Allen & Unwin).

Bolinger, D. (1946), 'Visual morphemes', *Language*, 22, pp. 333–40.

Bolinger, D. (1975), *Aspects of Language, 2nd edn* (New York: Harcourt, Brace & Jovanovich).

Chao, Y. R. (1968), *Language and Symbolic Systems*, Ch. 8 (Cambridge: C.U.P.), pp. 101–12.

Crystal, D. (1988), *The English Language* (Harmondsworth: Penguin).

Haas, W. (1970), *Phono-graphic Translation* (Manchester: Manchester University Press).

Haas, W. (ed.) (1976), *Writing Without Letters* (Manchester: Manchester University Press).

Halliday, M. A. K. (1989), *Spoken and Written English* (Oxford: O.U.P.).

Hockett, C. (1952), 'Speech and writing', *Georgetown Monograph*, No. 2, pp. 66–76.

Householder, F. W. (1971), 'The primacy of writing', in F. W. Householder, *Linguistic Speculations* (Cambridge: C.U.P.), pp. 244–64.

Kress, G. (1982), *Learning to Write* (London: Routledge & Kegan Paul).

Lunzer, E. and Gardner, K. (1979), *The Effective Use of Reading* (London: Heinemann Educational).

Pulgram, E. (1951), 'Phoneme and grapheme: a parallel', *Word*, 7, pp. 15–20.

Sampson, G. (1985), *Writing Systems* (London: Hutchinson).

Sanford, A. J. and Garrod, S. C. (1981), *Understanding Written Language: Explorations of Comprehension Beyond the Sentence* (Chichester: Wiley).

Stubbs, M. (1980), *The Sociolinguistics of Reading and Writing* (London: Routledge & Kegan Paul).

Todd, L. (1987), *An Introduction to Linguistics* (Harlow: Longman York Press).

2 Dialects, Accents and Standards

Most speakers of English, hearing someone say 'It gars ye fash', would not only not know what it meant, but might even find it difficult to identify the language being used. Similarly, few would be able to identify a 'ginnel', let us say, or a 'gation', or 'grouts'.

Yet all these expressions are English, and may even be said to be contemporary English since, though they are not all equally common, they are all current at the present time among monolingual speakers of English in different parts of Britain. Thus 'It gars ye fash' might be said by an elderly person living in a country district of central Scotland, to indicate annoyance with someone or something; 'ginnel' is the word frequently used in Leeds as the name of a narrow passage between houses; 'gation' is a very thin person in part of Northern Ireland; and 'grouts' are what people in the south-east of England leave in their cups when they have drunk their tea.

The reason why these expressions would be familiar to only a minority of English speakers is suggested by the phrase 'in different parts of Britain', for each expression occurs only in a relatively limited geographic area and is to be regarded, therefore, as a 'dialect' expression, rather than part of what is usually called 'Standard English'.

Not all dialect is as inaccessible to the majority of speakers as the expressions quoted. For example, the construction in which 'want' is followed by an active participle where a passive participle would be expected in Standard English (e.g. 'He wants his windows washing' for 'He wants his windows washed') would be readily understood by British speakers of English everywhere, though it is much more likely to be heard in certain parts of the north of England. Similarly 'She run', where Standard English would have 'She runs', would cause little difficulty outside the area of East Anglia where it is the regular form. Furthermore, there is a considerable area of overlap between dialect and Standard English, so that in many cases it would be foolish to suggest that a given grammatical device, say, belongs to one or the other, since it is common to both; for instance, the means of forming the plural.

Attitudes to dialect English vary. Some people regard it as deviant or substandard, intrinsically inferior to Standard English, which they tend to refer to as 'real' or 'proper' English. Others, perhaps a majority, would argue that dialect is more vigorous or livelier than Standard English. Judgements of this kind, however, judgements of value, really reveal more about the people making them than they do about dialect. Accordingly, we shall ignore them, and concern ourselves rather with such questions as: what is a dialect? what is a language? what is Standard English?

The best way to arrive at a proper understanding of the nature of dialect English is to begin by setting aside the fact that English can be written as well as spoken, and concentrating upon the spoken language. It is usually argued by scholars that Standard English is itself to be regarded as a dialect. If this is true, however, it has to be added that it is fundamentally different from all other dialects in a number of ways. In particular, it is unique, with the possible exception of literary Scots, in having its own writing system. When, as sometimes happens, writers attempt to reproduce dialect English in writing, they have to do so by adapting the conventions of the Standard English writing system. Dialect English, therefore, is characteristically spoken.

A dialect, or a language for that matter, is usually described in terms of three distinct, though interacting strata: the sound system, the vocabulary and the grammar. Dialect differences must also be dealt with in terms of these strata. Usually, of course, they do occur at all three levels, but variation at one level is *in principle* independent of variation at the other two. A difference at the sound system level, for example, does not necessarily entail a corresponding difference of vocabulary or grammar. It will be better, therefore, to discuss each stratum separately.

In discussions of dialect, the various elements of the sound system are usually subsumed in the general term 'accent', or perhaps 'pronunciation'. Unfortunately, both these terms tend to be somewhat misleading, in that both are popularly used with reference to sound quality, whereas in fact other aspects of the sound system, for example, the number of significant sound units that have to be recognised and the way these units occur relative to one another, are equally important in describing a particular sound system. Furthermore, both terms are popularly interpreted as referring to the individual sound segment; so that, for example, difference of accent between, say, Yorkshire and the south of England, is frequently exemplified by the different realisations of the vowel segment in such words as 'path', with other important differences elsewhere in the sound system being ignored. We shall continue to use the term 'accent' here, but with the proviso that it is to be understood as referring to the sound system as a whole.

Certainly, sound quality is the kind of accent feature most immediately apparent to the casual observer. Many speakers of English would probably be able to detect the difference between the Scottish and English pronunciations of, for example, 'like', 'smile' and 'fine', simply because, though both pronunciations realise the vowel segment as a glide (i.e. a diphthong), the distance between the first element of the glide and the last is much shorter in the Scottish version. Similarly, most native speakers would be able to detect, though perhaps not to identify, qualitative differences in other vowel segments, as between Scottish and English speakers; for example, in 'day', 'home', 'fool', 'foul' and 'port'. And since these differences extend to every word which includes the given vowel segment, the speech of the Scottish speaker is immediately recognisable.

Differences of quality also occur in the pronunciation of consonants; for example, the pronunciation of the initial consonant in 'run', 'right' and 'reel' varies according to region, as does the pronunciation of the middle consonant in, for example, 'butter', 'better' and 'water'. However, differences of quality are more frequent and more extensive in vowel segments.

The difference of pronunciation between Scottish 'like' and English 'like' may be regarded as significant in the sense that it may help to identify where a speaker comes from. But it is not functional, any more than the differences one finds in writing between different representations of the same letter; *a* and a, for example or r and *r*, or f and *f*. The pronunciation differences between, for example, 'pin' and 'pen', 'bin' and 'ben' and 'bit' and 'bet', on the other hand, *are* functional. Here the differences are comparable to those between different letters – a and e, p and b, r and q, for example – and so they enable speakers of the language to distinguish from one another words which refer to different objects in the real world.

This functional kind of sound difference is called a 'phonemic' difference. We do not have space here to explain precisely what 'phonemes' are, but broadly speaking they may be described as abstract functional units of the sound system. They are not themselves sound segments, since they are abstract, but every actual sound segment which occurs in speech must be identified with one or other of them in order to explain intelligibility in speech. Sometimes phonemes are described as 'families of sounds', because each abstract is associated with a variety of qualitatively different actual sounds. However, identification of the phonemes in a given language is not undertaken on the basis of similarity of sound between the members of the family, but rather on the basis of *contrast* with other families, i.e. phonemes.

For example, the *thing* 'pen' is a different kind of object from the *thing* 'pin'; hence, the *word* 'pen' is significantly different from the *word* 'pin'. Since the only way of distinguishing these two words from one another is by the different pronunciations of their vowel segments, the difference of pronunciation is a functional one; and so the vowel segments are assigned to different phonemes. It is on the basis of functional contrasts of this kind that an inventory of sound families, or phonemes, may be set up for any human language.

Both the number of phonemes and the membership of individual phonemes vary from language to language, and indeed, within a language, from dialect to dialect. Thus, for example, many Scottish accents rhyme 'father' and 'gather' and so fail to recognise a contrast common elsewhere in English. The same accents may also fail to distinguish 'cot' from 'caught', and 'pool' from 'pull', and Scottish accents, therefore, have a smaller vowel inventory than many other accents of English. Similarly, some American accents do not distinguish 'bomb' and 'balm', some northern English accents sound 'cud' and 'could' alike, and a Cockney pronounces 'thin' like 'fin'. Sounding Scottish, or American, or Irish, or Yorkshire, or whatever, is not merely a matter of superficial differences of sound quality, then, but more fundamentally of differences in the phoneme inventory with which each operates.

Moreover, even where the same phoneme does occur in different dialects, it may be distributed differently in each. Thus, for example, /r/ occurs in all English accents, though as we saw earlier there are qualitative differences in its realisation from region to region. But despite the fact that it occurs in every dialect, it is not used everywhere in the same way. For instance, many accents of English do have some kind of /r/ in 'bird', 'farm', 'near' and 'her', for example, but in the east and south-east of England this sound does not occur in such words, i.e. before a consonant, or finally in the word. In common with all other accents of English, however, these accents do have /r/ between vowels and initially in the word; for example, in 'marry', 'berry', 'red' and 'road'. Many other examples of a similar kind could be given.

Though the system of phonemic contrasts is an important part of the sound system of any language, it is by no means the whole story. There are other, equally important elements. There are, for example, three very important systems based on a unit of a different kind from the phoneme; the unit of intonation, called the 'tone group'.

One of these intonation systems has to do with the choice of boundary for the tone group. Thus 'old men, and women', where 'old' applies only to 'men', is pronounced as two tone groups, with a slight pause between 'men' and 'and', shown in writing by a comma; whereas 'old men and women', with 'old' applying to both 'men' and 'women', has to be just one tone group. In the same way we distinguish between 'The passengers who wore lifebelts were saved' and 'The passengers, who wore lifebelts, were saved'. In the latter case only, 'who wore lifebelts' is a separate tone group, the other sentence being spoken as one tone group. The difference of meaning is that the first sentence asserts that only some passengers were saved; the second that all passengers were saved.

A second intonation system determines which syllable in a tone group will receive the main stress. For example, the written sentence 'Mary shot the burglar' may give different information, i.e. mean different things, according to which syllable receives the strong stress. If the first syllable of 'burglar' is stressed, the sentence answers the question 'Who did Mary shoot?'; if 'shot' is stressed, then the original question asked 'How did Mary kill the burglar?'; and if 'Mary' is stressed, the original question was probably 'Who shot the burglar?'.

The last of the three intonation systems is concerned with choice of speech melody, that is, with significant pitch sequences, within a tone group. For example, the reader will be aware that it is possible to change a statement into a question simply by an alteration in the pitch sequence. There are, however, less obvious possibilities. Thus, the written sentence 'I didn't like him because of his good looks' is ambiguous. In speech, this ambiguity is resolved and the hearer understands the sentence to mean either 'I did not like him, and the reason was his good looks' or 'I liked him, but not because of his good looks', according to which speech melody the speaker uses. These melodies are very difficult to display in writing, unfortunately, but readers might like to try for themselves whether they are able to make a similar distinction; for example with 'I wasn't annoyed because he was on time', or 'She didn't go because you were there'.

These three systems are very complex and we certainly cannot describe them in detail here. But we have pointed to their existence in order to draw attention to the fact that virtually nothing is known concerning how they enter into dialect differences. It is possible that the first two systems may be more or less identical throughout the whole of English; though if this is so, it is something we should like to know for certain. The third system, on the other hand, that which is concerned with selection of the appropriate speech melody, is clearly involved in dialect difference. Even an untrained ear can detect, for example, that the actual speech melodies used vary from place to place, so that the melodies heard in the speech of Glasgow speakers are unlike those heard in Birmingham, say, or Cardiff, or even Edinburgh. But how far the difference between dialects is merely one involving a change of melody, and how far it involves something more fundamental (so that one person's question, let us say, sounds like another's statement) is impossible to say, for none of the 'tone group' systems has been systematically studied from the dialect point of view.

Yet another aspect of the sound system which is neglected so far as dialect studies are concerned is the way in which such factors as loudness, tempo, speech melody, either singly or in combination, communicate certain kinds of meaning relating to the attitude of the speaker. Thus, most of us are able to perceive when someone speaking in our native accent is being sympathetic, say, or contemptuous, or suspicious, or aggressive, or deferential. We are able, that is, to interpret the implications of 'tone of voice'. Just how we do this has never been studied in detail, though the question is raised from time to time by phoneticians, and the factors involved are fairly well understood at a general level. But what has not been investigated in depth is how dialects differ from one another with respect to this phenomenon.

That they do differ is clear. Thus, fairly neutral statements in certain west of Scotland accents appear to outsiders to have a whining quality, while in other Scottish accents they would appear aggressive or argumentative. Slow, apparently more melodious accents, such as those heard in East

Anglia or Devon, are usually felt by outsiders to indicate an easy-going nature, but are not infrequently associated also with simple-mindedness. The stage has made use of this stereotyping for centuries. However, most of the evidence in this area is anecdotal and impressionistic. Everyone is aware of this dimension in dialect differences, but perhaps because of the difficulties involved, nobody has studied it thoroughly.

Difficulties are, presumably, relatively fewer when it comes to the study of vocabulary differences. At any rate, it is this aspect of dialect variation which is most popular with researchers, both professional and amateur, and it is this aspect, consequently, about which most is known.

Present vocabulary differences, like all dialect differences, have their roots in the past, and often a long way back in the past. Some go back to differences which already existed when the Angles, Saxons and Jutes began to arrive on the shores of Britain. Naturally, since they were probably illiterate, evidence concerning the dialect position is wanting; and even later, during the literate period, the evidence is scanty and fragmentary. Nevertheless, where we now find different contemporary terms with clearly regional distribution, and where these modern terms are descended from different Old English terms, then one reasonable inference is that the present distributional difference may reflect a difference which was there in Old English, that is pre-Conquest, times; though of course, not necessarily with exactly the same regional currency.

For purposes of illustration we may take the various terms used to name the building where cows were kept. There are, in fact, quite a number. In southern Scotland and parts of Ireland, and northern England, the name generally given to this building was 'byre' (OE bȳre). In north-west England, parts of Yorkshire, Derbyshire, Staffordshire and Shropshire, and in a separate area covering Devon, part of Cornwall and part of Somerset, the word used was 'shippon' (OE scypen). West Yorkshire had 'mistall' (OE meox + steall); north Suffolk and south Norfolk, 'neat-house' (OE nēat + hūs); and the west of Warwickshire, 'cow-pen' (OE cū + penn). Elsewhere, apart from one or two small areas where the terms used derive from Old French, people used 'cow-house' or 'cow-shed' (OE cū + hūs or scēad). These last two terms seem to be spreading at the expense of the others. In particular, it appears that 'shippon' originally had a much wider distribution, and that the two small areas where it is found now are all that is left of a much larger area which included them both. As for 'byre', it seems reasonable to conclude that this term also had wider distribution, in fact the old kingdom of Northumbria, which stretched from the Humber to the Forth.

Another ancient source of present difference is Old Norse, the language of the Scandinavian invaders of Britain. For instance, in southern Scotland and northern England, down as far as north Yorkshire and Lancashire, people attended the 'kirk' (ON kirkja) on Sunday, whereas elsewhere they went to 'church' (OE cirice). Similarly, northerners made their butter in a 'kirn' (ON kirna), while southerners used a 'churn' (OE cyren) for this purpose; northerners wore a 'sark' (ON serkr), whereas southerners made do with a 'shirt' (OE serce); northerners crossed a 'brig' (ON bryggja), but southerners crossed a 'bridge' (OE brycg); a northerner might 'loup' (ON hlaupa) where a southerner would 'leap' (OE hlēapan).

French is also a cause of vocabulary differences. Thus, over most of England the implement used to sweep the house is called a 'brush' (O.Fr. broisse), in contrast with 'broom' (OE brōm), which is used in an area stretching down diagonally from the west midlands to Kent and Sussex, and up into the southern part of East Anglia. Similarly we have England split between 'beasts' (O.Fr. beste) and 'cattle' (old Norman Fr. catel); and in some areas a visitor would be entertained in the 'parlour' (O.Fr. parleor), while elsewhere he would be received in the 'room' (OE rūm), or the 'sitting-room' (OE sittan) or 'front-room' (O.Fr. front).

Another possible source of vocabulary difference among dialects is human fondness for novelty. Someone bestows a new name upon a familiar object, perhaps as a joke, and the new name catches the popular fancy and spreads. For example, the term 'cuddy' used in the north of England for 'donkey' is a shortened form of 'Cuthbert'. Elsewhere we find 'dicky' (short for Richard), 'neddy' (short for Edward), 'moke', 'fussock', 'pronkus' and 'nirrup', none of which has the slightest connection with either the OE 'assa' (modern ass), or with the most popular modern form 'donkey', which may itself be a product of the same kind of inventiveness. Other probable examples of dialectal inventiveness are: 'coochy-' or 'cuddy-handed', for 'left-handed'; 'mawkin' (a diminutive from 'Maud'), for 'scarecrow'; 'tabs', for 'ears'; and 'Old Nick', for 'the devil'.

So far we have been discussing cases where the thing remains constant while the word differs from place to place. But, of course, it often happens that words exist in one dialect which are lacking in others, simply because the things to which the words refer are purely local. When the British first arrived in North America, for example, they found there many things for which they had no names. Often they adopted the Indian name: 'racoon', 'skunk', 'moose', 'canoe', for example. In other cases they made use of the possibility offered by English for such new formations as 'mud hen', 'garter snake' and 'ground hog'. Then, as they came into contact with other European immigrants they occasionally adopted their terms: 'bayou', 'levee', 'prairie', from French, for example; 'pretzel', from German; 'cookie' and 'stoop' from Dutch; and 'burro', 'corral', 'mesa', 'bronco', and many others from Spanish.

Similarly, one finds vocabulary differences which result from difference of occupation or industry. For example, people living in mining areas are very likely to use terms relating to conditions and customs in the mining industry which have little or no currency outside those areas. Nor, indeed, will the terms necessarily remain the same from region to region within a particular industry. As the conditions and customs may vary from place to place even within the same occupation, it is not to be wondered at if the terms by which they are referred to also vary.

Finally, we may note that certain vocabulary differences are the other way around: the word remains the same but the thing is different. For instance, 'dinner' means the mid-day meal to some, but the evening meal to others; 'tea' is an afternoon meal in England but may be the early morning meal in Jamaica; a 'bucket' in parts of Scotland is a dustbin, whereas in England a 'bucket' is a pail; a 'backward' child in Northern Ireland is merely shy, elsewhere the word means 'retarded'; a 'chapel' in southern Scotland is a place of worship for Catholics, but in England usually for Methodists; 'robin' identifies entirely different birds in England, the USA and Australia; a 'crumpet' in Scotland is a round, flat, sweetened cake, similar to what in England is called a 'pancake', but a 'crumpet' in England is a round, flat, unsweetened cake; and, of course, Scottish 'cookies' differ both in shape and taste from American 'cookies'. The list of such differences is potentially very large indeed.

Other kinds of vocabulary difference do undoubtedly exist between dialects. However, those we have briefly considered above are probably the main types. They will suffice, in any case, to illustrate a very important point: regional differences of vocabulary are neither mysterious nor reprehensible. On the contrary, they are entirely natural and to be expected. No human language could, and no human language does, exist without them.

Moreover, though we lack space to demonstrate it here, the same holds true for the other two strata: variant modern forms arise from legitimate earlier forms for natural and well-understood reasons. There is really no objective basis for preferring one set of variants over another. All dialects are intrinsically equal. Most of us are aware of preferences, and sometimes we are prepared to give them considerable weight, but our preferences are really completely subjective and should, if we are honest, be regarded rather in the nature of prejudices.

We turn now to the third stratum of language description: grammar. In simple terms we can say that grammar has two main branches: morphology and syntax. The former is concerned with the systematic alterations in the forms of words by which English – since we are dealing here with English – signals such grammatical categories as person, number and tense, as well as with the study of the ways in which English words may be formed; by the use of prefixes or suffixes, for example. The other branch of grammar, syntax, is concerned with the way in which sentences are constructed out of smaller units; and so it takes in such matters as phrase, clause and sentence structure, co-ordination and subordination, mood and transitivity. With regard to dialect studies, morphology has been fairly extensively researched and recorded; syntax considerably less so.

Among nouns there appears to be relatively little to note. There are a few words which are regularly found in particular areas with archaic plurals; for example, 'een' (eyes), 'shin' (shoes), 'kye' (cows) occur regularly in southern Scotland. Another dialect phenomenon affecting nouns is the tendency to derive new singular forms from apparent plurals. Thus, in Northern Ireland, for example, we may find 'Chinee' (as singular of 'Chinese'), 'corp' (as singular of 'corpse') and 'barrack' (as singular of 'barracks'). There is also a dialect usage whereby nouns relating to time, weight or measure do not add the expected -s in the plural: 'two pound', 'three score', 'five shilling', 'six pair', 'four year'. And, in a few areas nouns ending in -sk, -sp, or -st add -es to form their plurals: 'caskes', 'waspes', 'postes'. Apart from these, differences are few and sporadic.

Differences are more frequent and more noticeable with verbs. Thus, some dialects, Cockney among them, regularly add -s to the first singular, present: 'I walks to work every day'; 'I likes my pipe'. By contrast, in East Anglia it is regular to have a third singular, present, lacking final -s: 'He walk to work'; 'He sleep late regular(ly)'. With the past tense and past participle forms differences appear to be even more extensive. Thus, in some areas of Britain and America we find examples like the following: 'beat', past 'bet', past participle 'bet'; 'help, holp, holp'; 'sit, set, set'; 'swell, swole, swole'; 'take, took, took'; 'tear, tore, tore'; 'blow, blowed, blowed'; 'know, knowed, knowed'.

Differences are also to be found affecting prepositions. In East Anglia, for example, we find 'I'm not afraid on 'im', with 'on' for standard 'of'. In various parts of the USA a son may be called 'after' his father, or, with the same meaning, 'at', 'from', or 'for' his father. Conjunction usage may also vary; for example, 'while' occurs for 'till' in the north and east of England and in the north midlands, giving such potentially ambiguous sentences as 'You won't learn anything while (until) you listen to me'. Not even adjectives and adverbs are immune; use of the adjective form adverbially is common, for example, so that we may find 'He hasn't done bad' or 'Elvis sang real good'. However, the most extensive differences are undoubtedly to be found among the pronouns.

Thus, for example, among the personal pronouns 'I' may occur as object: 'He saw I'; 'They told I'. For the second person forms we have a variety of possibilities: 'thee' as object; 'thou' as subject in the singular; 'ye' or 'ee' as subject, object, singular and plural; and in many areas a distinction between 'you' (sing.) and 'youse' (pl.). For the third singular we find, for example, 'that' instead of 'it' in East Anglia, as in 'That's raining'; 'hit' for 'it' in the north and in Scotland; 'en' or ''n' (from OE 'hine'), for 'him', especially in the south-west; 'he' and 'she' as object forms, and 'him' and 'her' as subject forms. In the first, plural, 'us' may occur instead of 'we', and conversely; and in the third plural 'them' and 'they' may similarly interchange.

Among the possessives there are differences in both pronouns and adjectives. Thus, in both Britain and the USA one can find 'hisn', 'hern', 'ourn', 'yourn' and 'theirn' occurring as possessive pronouns, presumably by analogy with 'mine'. In West Yorkshire and the West Midlands 'us' occurs as the first plural possessive adjective. 'Give us us books', for example; and we also find 'thy', corresponding to 'thee/thou'. Elsewhere we have 'his' or 'it' for 'its', and sometimes a periphrastic avoidance of 'its' by means of a construction with 'of', e.g. 'the tail of it' for 'its tail'.

Demonstratives also exhibit dialect differences. Thus, in Scotland and Northern Ireland 'them' occurs regularly for 'those'; and 'thon' for both 'that' and 'those' (and there is a corresponding adverb 'thonder'). In many parts of the English-speaking world 'they' and 'them' occur as demonstratives ('Gimme them boots'), and also 'this here' and 'that there': while further south and west we find 'thick', 'thicky' and similar forms (from ME thilke).

Dialectologists have on the whole steered clear of syntax. This is not, perhaps, altogether surprising, for syntax tended to be neglected by grammarians until relatively recently. Even so, enough has been done to demonstrate that differences exist between dialects at this stratum also.

With regard to subordination, for example, avoidance of the relative pronouns 'who' and 'whom' is widespread in dialect English. Frequently the pronoun is omitted completely: 'I know a man will do it for you'. Otherwise we may find 'as', 'that' or 'what': 'I know a man as (that/what) has ten cows'. We may also encounter 'as what' and 'like what' used as subordinating conjunctions; 'You're as bad as what he is', 'He don't sing like what he used to'. Another widespread form is 'for to', in constructions such as 'I decided for to tell him'. Less widespread, but still fairly common, 'seeing as how' and 'being as' occur as subordinating conjunctions with the meaning 'because' or 'since': 'Seeing as how (being as) he's late, we'll start without him'.

Subordination is not the only area where syntactical differences occur. For instance, in a number of areas, including southern Scotland, northern England, Northern Ireland and Australia, there is a curious use of 'but' at the end of a sentence; as in 'He'll be angry, but'. Evidently 'but' is here no longer a co-ordinating conjunction but is added in order to give some kind of emphasis. Perhaps even more alien to the orthodox ear, though it is certainly not rare, is the multiple negative: 'Nobody don't go there no more'. Despite the fact that it is firmly condemned by traditional grammarians, there really are no reasonable grounds for rejecting this construction. Indeed, Shakespeare uses multiple negation in Sonnet 116:

If this be error, and upon me prov'd,
I never writ, nor no man ever lov'd.

Equally archaic-sounding, though perhaps less objectionable to the purist is the dialect usage of an imperative with explicit second-person object, as in 'Go you off home at once', and even 'Cut you me a piece of bread'; or the northern use of an active participle where Standard English has a passive; 'Does he want his car servicing?'.

Finally, as the reader will no doubt have realised, the examples given above of phonological, lexical and grammatical variation are not offered as a comprehensive account of dialect diversity, but are intended rather as illustration and exemplification of the nature and extent of that diversity.

Thus far we have really been concerned with the question of *how* English may vary. We must now consider the related question of *why*; in other words, the identification of those external, non-language factors to which variation appears to respond. In fact we may recognise at least seven such factors:

(1)   individuality
(2)   region
(3)   class
(4)   participant factors (including role and purpose)
(5)   topic
(6)   setting
(7)   other language activity.

Of these, the first three relate to the kind of variation we can call 'dialect'; the others to variation of 'style', which will be discussed in a separate chapter.

Dialect diversity begins with the individual; for though most of us are unaware of the fact, or alternatively choose to ignore it, no two of us speak exactly the same language. This is so whatever language we claim to speak: each one of us has a personal dialect, or 'idiolect', as it is called.

Idiolects represent a complication and an inconvenience to the language scholar, who is interested primarily in the language of groups (of varying size). Clearly, if everyone in a group speaks a different variety of their language, the task of describing the language of the group becomes enormously difficult. Dialectologists have tended to deal with the problem by ignoring it; so that, for example, they are prepared to accept the speech of one individual as representative of a fairly large district. Linguists, on the other hand, have developed theoretical devices which supposedly eliminate the diversity. The distinction made by the founder of modern linguistics, Ferdinand de Saussure, between 'langue' and 'parole', was a device of this kind; as is the distinction between 'competence' and 'performance' made by the American linguist Noam Chomsky.

But whether it is theoretically recognised or not, the reality of language is not homogeneity, but continuous diversity. For example, we are all able to recognise the voices of a very large number of individuals on the telephone. There is always something – in the pitch, in the quality of the sounds produced, in the intonation – which is unique and which enables us to tell one from the other. Sometimes differences may be very small, as they are, normally, with twins. But even twins are sufficiently different to be distinguished by close relatives and friends.

Idiolectal vocabulary differences include different pronunciations of individual words. Among those the reader may have noted are the alternative forms of 'often' (with and without /t/); of 'electric' (beginning with /i/ and /ɪ/); of 'questionnaire' (beginning /kɛs-/ and /kwɛs-/); and 'harass' (with the stress on either the first or the second syllable).

Also frequent is the use of different words for the same thing, on an individual basis. An excellent example is the many possible alternatives to the word 'lavatory': 'toilet', 'loo', 'bog', 'john', 'WC', 'whatsit', 'heads', and 'latrines'. Other obvious ways in which individuals may differ from one another is in the word they use when they have failed to hear something: 'excuse me', 'sorry', 'pardon (me)', 'what?', 'eh?'; in the way they greet friends: 'hello', 'hi', 'wotcher', 'howdy', 'nathen', 'good morning/ afternoon'; in their drinking salutations: 'good health', 'cheers', 'down the hatch'; or in their mild swear words: 'blow', 'blast', 'damn', 'hell' or 'knickers'; to mention only a few differences that the reader can easily amplify.

Beyond this we find words occurring in the vocabulary of one individual but not in that of another. For example, the expression 'capitalist press' would be unlikely to occur in the vocabulary of a supporter of that institution; just as 'lefty' would not usually occur in the vocabulary of one who could be so described. Many people would avoid using words like 'nasty', 'naughty', or 'wicked' because they would regard them as too 'namby-pamby'; and for a different reason, some would avoid 'mistress' or 'lover'. Then, of course, there are individuals who have favourite words which the majority of the population never use, and do not properly understand; words such as 'penumbra', 'nebulous', 'permeate', or 'pernicious'.

Possibly the most noticeable individual difference concerns not words but phrases. We seem to become fond of particular phrases and to use them so regularly that they come to act as a kind of signature tune. President Bush, for example, often used the Clint Eastwood expression 'Make my day!' in his 1988 Election Campaign. And doubtless the reader will recognise one or other of the following favourites: 'I want to be alone', 'Come up and see me sometime', 'You dirty rat!', 'Hello possums' or 'Know what I mean, 'Arry?'. It is an interesting exercise, in fact, to note the favourites of our acquaintances and of ourselves.

Grammatical idiolectal differences are a bit more difficult to pin down. Nevertheless, they do occur. For example, one finds individuals who favour '-wise' as an adverb-forming suffix, as in 'salary-wise', 'holiday-wise', 'work-wise'. And the reader may well note in the work of some writers a characteristic fondness for 'moreover', 'furthermore' and 'however' as introductory sentence adverbs. It is possible to observe, also, individual differences in such things as the use of relative pronouns (as between 'the man who I saw', 'the man whom I saw' and 'the man I saw'); in a fondness for subordination in preference to co-ordination; the use of a noun instead of a clause with a similar meaning ('his behaviour' rather than 'the way he behaves'); and, in fact, wherever there are alternative possibilities some will favour one, some another.

We may note in passing that the idiolect is itself subject to internal variation with time. We all add new items to our vocabulary from time to time and let others go out of use; we modify our pronunciation in response to non-linguistic influences such as change of residence or of status; and our individual grammar acquires new constructions and relinquishes old ones. (See also under 'Style', Chapter 4, for another kind of idiolectal variety.) The characteristic of human languages even at the level of the idiolect, therefore, is constant diversity.

Regional diversity takes over from individual diversity. The two are not different in essence, but in degree. Each of us is, in a real sense, in contact with every other speaker of our language. With some, relatively few, we are in regular direct contact; with others, again, we are in contact irregularly and/ or indirectly, through intermediary contacts of various kinds; and, of course, we only contact the great majority through a whole complex of intermediate individuals and groups. Through this complex of intermediary contacts, small differences between individuals in close regular contact grow and extend until they may become large enough to render two people who claim to speak the same language mutually incomprehensible; as, say, a Kentucky hillbilly and a Scottish crofter. Regional diversity, thus, multiplies individual diversity.

This point is crucially important to a correct understanding of the nature of dialect. What we have, in effect, is a continuum of variation, starting from the individual and gradually extending throughout the entire population of those who speak the language.

In order to illustrate this by a concrete example, we have tabulated (Table 1) the occurrences throughout Yorkshire (Map 1) of a small number of dialect expressions as these are recorded in the *Survey of English Dialects (SED)*, Volume 1, Parts 1, 2 and 3. The items in question are as follows:

Ask, 4.9.8; elsewhere: newt, asker, eft.
Awns (i.e. horns), 2.5.3; elsewhere: whiskers, husks, beards.
Brambles, 4.11.1; elswhere: blackberries, brumble-kites, blags, etc.
Byre, 1.1.8; elsewhere: cow-house, shippon, mistall.
Cuddy, 3.13.16; elsewhere: donkey, fussock, moke, neddy.
Flay-crow, 2.3.7; elsewhere: scarecrow, mawpin, mawkin.
Gesling, 4.6.17; elswhere: gosling.
Haigs, 4.11.6; elsewhere: haws, cat-haws, haigins.
Nostrils, 6.4.7; elsewhere: nose-holes.
Ticks, 4.8.3; elsewhere: cades, lice.
Till (e.g. till Saturday), 9.2.2; elsewhere: while, to.
Urchin, 4.5.5; elsewhere: hedgehog, prickly-pig.

	Brambles	Byre	Cuddy	Haigs	Till	Gesling	Urchin	Ticks	Nostrils	Awns	Ask	Flay-Crow
1 Melsonby		+	+			+	+	+	+	+	+	+
2 Stokesley	+	+				+	+			+		+
3 Skelton		+	+			+	+		+	+	+	+
4 Egton							+			+		+
5 Dent						+	+					
6 Muker			+			+	+	+		+		+
7 Askrigg	+					+	+	+	+		+	
8 Bedale	+	+					+		+	+		+
9 Borrowby		+				+	+	+	+	+	+	+
10 Helmsley	+					+		+	+	+	+	+
11 Rillington	+					+	+	+		+		
12 Burton-in-Lonsdale	+					+	+	+	+	+		+
13 Horton-in-Ribblesdale							+	+			+	
14 Grassington	+		+									+
15 Pately Bridge							+	+		+	+	+
16 Easingwold	+						+	+	+	+		
17 Gargrave				+	+	+						
18 Spofforth	+						+			+		
19 York	+	+					+					+
20 Nafferton	+					+		+	+	+		
21 Heptonstall				+	+						+	+
22 Wibsey				+	+	+			+			+
23 Leeds				+	+				+			
24 Cawood						+	+			+		+
25 Newbald	+					+	+		+	+		
26 Thornhill						+			+	+		
27 Carleton				+	+			+		+		
28 Welwick	+					+	+		+			
29 Golcar				+	+							+
30 Holmbridge				+	+	+	+			+		
31 Skelmanthorpe				+				+				
32 Ecclesfield	+			+	+					+	+	
33 Tickhill	+			+	+					+	+	
34 Sheffield					+				+			

Table 1   *Distribution of twelve vocabulary items in Yorkshire*

The number given for each item refers to the appropriate question in the *SED* questionnaire, published in the *Introduction* to *The Survey of English Dialects*.

Map 1   *Locations of SED informants in Yorkshire area*

The number of items tabulated is very small; twelve in all. Nevertheless, the table shows considerable diversity in the distribution of these twelve items. Moreover, with the sole exception of locations 32 and 33, Ecclesfield and Tickhill, no two of the locations listed yield exactly the same selection of these twelve items.

Thus, for example, if we move a few miles to the west of Leeds, to Wibsey, we find three items recorded which are not recorded for Leeds; while one of those recorded at Leeds is missing from Wibsey. A few miles to the east of Leeds, at Cawood, we find four items which are not recorded for Leeds; and one of those recorded at Leeds is absent. Similarly, at Spofforth, north of Leeds, and Thornhill, to the south, we have vocabularies which differ from Leeds, and from one another, with regard to several of the listed items.

It should be noted with regard to the *Survey of English Dialects* that little account was taken of the distinction between idiolectal and dialectal diversity. Indeed, since each response is recorded from a single informant for each locality, it could be said that the survey was, in effect, a survey of English idiolects. In the case of any given response, therefore, we must be unsure as to whether it represents the dialect of the district or merely the idiolect of the informant, and hence some at least of the diversity recorded in the speech of Yorkshire is undoubtedly attributable to individual rather than regional preference. For this very reason, however, the data tabulated make it clear that individual diversity extends eventually into regional diversity and, moreover, that the diversity is continuous.

Clearly, all this raises the question of whether it is proper to speak of, for example, 'the Yorkshire dialect' (or the Welsh dialect, or the New England dialect). One possibility would be to identify the dialect physically, so that the Yorkshire dialect, say, would be identified as the dialect spoken by native inhabitants of Yorkshire. However, the definition of 'dialect' implied by such identification would be linguistically arbitrary, and would, in addition, obscure both the internal diversity and the external continuity.

Alternatively, it might be argued that it is possible to define a particular regional dialect by reference to a small number of characteristic features which appear to be constant throughout the region in question. This, in fact, is probably how 'dialects' are popularly identified; so that speakers of Scots dialect are recognised by the way they pronounce /r/, let us say, or replace English 'night' by 'nicht'. However, once again, if we proceed in this way we lose sight of the reality; for the reality is that even Scots is internally diverse, and externally continuous. Furthermore, as we shall see later, not everyone who uses a Scots pronunciation is speaking Scots dialect. It is clearly possible to identify the regional provenance of *speakers* by reference to a small number of key pronunciation features, but it is extremely doubtful whether it is either possible or desirable to attempt to define *dialects* in the same way.

Another possibility is provided by the fact that though dialect diversity is continuous, and for the most part gradual, it is not uniform. Sometimes several differences occur close together and give a rough line along which the density of difference is relatively greater than it is on either side. This becomes apparent if isoglosses, or boundary lines, are drawn round the areas where individual features occur. Most of the isoglosses will be seen to occur randomly with respect to one another, thus giving a picture of continuous diversity; as is the case with the features tabulated in Table 1. But a few isoglosses may roughly coincide with one another, and this coincidence may be regarded as identifying dialect boundaries. This is how traditional dialectologists distinguish one dialect area from another. For example, in the north of England there is a rough correspondence of the line between 'grew' and 'growed' and that between 'knew' and 'knowed', as the past tense forms of 'grow' and 'know' respectively. Also roughly corresponding are the boundary lines for a number of vocabulary forms.

The bundle of isoglosses resulting may be regarded as marking the southern limits of Danish influence and hence of the Northern dialect of English.

Nevertheless, it has to be emphasised that the correspondence between isoglosses is never better than approximate (even if we could assume that they are always accurate). In any case, the number of isoglosses which can be 'bundled' in this way is relatively small. Bundles of isoglosses, therefore, do not indicate a break in the continuity of change but only a local fluctuation in its uniformity.

The diversity of the dialect continuum is subject to modification in other ways. It is affected, first of all, by the existence of large conurbations such as London, New York and Sydney, which seem to generate their own characteristic kind of diversity. Factors such as the density of population and the variety of roles people are called upon to fill, while they do not break the continuity, do alter its character. In particular, social class differences seem to assume a greater importance in some urban contexts and introduce new complexities into the dialect situation. We shall have more to say on class dialect later, when we come to consider the class factor in more detail.

Another factor which may affect the nature of the dialect continuum is the kind of geographical feature, such as a mountain, a river, or a lake, which by interrupting the physical continuity of speakers of the language may be thought to interrupt the dialect continuum itself.

Such interruption may, indeed, occur, as it occurred when the Angles, Saxons and Jutes settled in the British Isles. When they first arrived, their speech was part of a Germanic dialect continuum which also included the ancestors of Modern Dutch, Frisian and Low German. It did not cease to be part of that linguistic continuum merely because the physical continuity of speakers was interrupted by the North Sea. As time passed, because of the effect of a variety of factors, such as the Viking and French invasions and the lack of regular contact with continental speakers of related dialects, the linguistic continuum was also interrupted and English emerged as a separate language.

It should be noted in passing that though the assertion that English became a separate language would raise few eyebrows, it is in fact virtually impossible to find objective criteria in terms of which it would be possible to define either the process of separation itself, or the point at which that process might be regarded as complete. The point is that in a continuum of variation, just as it is impossible satisfactorily to identify individual dialects, so it is equally impossible to distinguish a dialect from a language. The usual rule of thumb offered to identify the point at which a dialect becomes a separate language is *mutual incomprehensibility*; that is, speakers of different dialects may be regarded as speaking different languages when they are no longer able to understand one another. Incomprehensibility, however, is clearly an unsatisfactory criterion. Not only is it a matter of degree, but it varies from individual to individual and even from context to context; so that a certain degree of intelligibility in, say, the market place is no guarantee of the ability to carry on an intelligible conversation. Moreover, it is quite common for speakers of a regional dialect to understand speakers of Standard English, who are unable to understand them. And, in any case, it is not difficult to find dialects of English which, though they are mutually incomprehensible, are yet regarded as part of the same continuum, and so still dialects and not separate languages.

Nor would it improve matters to rely on formal criteria as a means of defining separation, either as a process or as a state. Formal criteria are themselves acceptably objective, but there is simply no way of deciding objectively just how many formal features must differ, and by how much, before separation might be judged to have occurred; or even whether all features are equally significant. Furthermore, separate languages do sometimes become recognised even when no break in linguistic continuity occurs. For example, a dialect continuum stretches through Holland into Germany, unbroken by the political frontier by reference to which a division into two separate languages is made.

Despite difficulties of definition, however, it is clear that the migration of people across the North Sea did eventually result in the emergence of a distinct language; or, more correctly, a distinct dialect continuum. Surprisingly, perhaps, later migrations of the British have not had the same effect. No new languages have developed. (See, however, Chapter 3: Pidgins and Creoles.)

Unquestionably, early settlements, particularly in North America, must have existed in conditions at least superficially similar to those experienced by the first English-speaking immigrants to Britain. The settlements in both cases would have been small and relatively isolated from one another; contact with the native population, even where it was friendly, could hardly have been intimate, because of fundamental social and linguistic differences; and contact with the homeland would have been sporadic, and probably one-way, because of the difficulties of travel. Moreover, when settlements began to expand and link up with one another, the result was the creation of a dialect continuum in North America, just as it had been in Britain.

But if there were obvious similarities between the two sets of circumstances there were also important differences. One such difference must have been a factor encouraging separation of North American English from British English, for the North American settler must have been under much greater pressure than his earlier British counterpart to develop his language both lexically and grammatically in order to be able to talk about the strange people, animals, plants and natural phenomena that he encountered in his new surroundings. Britain was, after all, not very different from the European homeland, whereas America was a whole new world. And yet North American English did not separate; and this was without doubt because of two even more powerful factors operating in the opposite direction.

The first of these arose from the fact that whereas the early Germanic settlers in Britain were really only marauding tribesmen moving from one territory to another and recognising allegiance to nobody but themselves, the North American settlers were colonists for a powerful nation-state, to which they were entitled to look for protection, but which in return demanded allegiance and, above all, trade. The immigrant to Britain, therefore, probably settled into his new home without, as it were, a backward glance: to the British settler in North America, on the other hand, Britain continued for many generations to be 'home', and contact was thus not only assured but encouraged.

The crucial factor in preventing a separation of overseas English from British English after the later migrations was not the maintenance of political and commercial ties, however, important as these undoubtedly were; it was the existence of a standard version of the language. To understand why this was so we must look at the way Standard English developed, what it is and how it functions.

In the fourteenth century, English existed *only* as a continuum of dialects. The amount of variation was considerable; so much so that though everybody could claim to be speaking English, individual speakers could count on being easily understood by only a minority of their countrymen: those brought up near enough to have acquired a variety not too different from their own. The language was written as well as spoken, but each scribe did his best to represent his own local variety of spoken English, using scribal conventions partly handed down from Old English times and partly learned from French. Indeed, our knowledge of the dialect situation at this period depends upon the variation apparent in the written language accurately reflecting that in the spoken.

After the beginning of the fifteenth century English replaced French and Latin more and more as the language of official business. Most of this was conducted in London, but the striking fact is that by the early sixteenth century even documents which originated elsewhere, such as wills and charters, were usually written in the dialect used by London administrators. This variety of English is referred to in *A Linguistic Atlas of Late Medieval English* (McIntosh *et al.*) as 'Chancery Standard'.

Such a development meant, in effect, that provincial scribes were obliged to acquire a variety of English which was in many respects different from their local speech. Moreover, perhaps because its association with important documents gave the official written form greater prestige than any locally based variety, its use was before long extended to other forms of writing, including literature and, later, English versions of the Bible. No doubt this trend was encouraged by the arrival in London, towards the end of the fifteenth century, of printing, which for the first time made possible wide distribution of written texts. So it was that by the early sixteenth century, wherever in England one lived, and whatever variety of English one spoke, being literate meant being able to read and write this originally very localised variety. Scotland, it is true, developed its own distinct written standard, but this was replaced by the English standard at the time of the Reformation.

The emergence of a written standard had important consequences. First, since literacy is essential to formal education, the grammar and vocabulary of the standard dialect had to be taught in schools. It was not, it is important to note, necessary to teach any particular accent. Since the use of the standard was primarily associated with writing the question of a standard pronunciation did not arise.

It is in the nature of things that writing attracts more prestige than speech, and so before long the grammar and vocabulary of the written standard came to be regarded as *correct* English, to be recommended in speech as in writing. It is a commonplace of linguistics that speech precedes writing historically, but with a standard language the development is commonly in the other direction, with regional spoken dialect being replaced, or at least complemented, by a spoken variety acquired through writing and school instruction.

The extension of the grammar and vocabulary of writing to the spoken language was facilitated by the absence of any standard accent, since this meant the language could be correctly spoken with the regional accent. A situation thus developed in which an increasing number of people learned to use Standard English in speech – albeit with a regional accent, perhaps slightly modified – as well as in writing. It is very likely, of course, that most such people would continue to use their regional variety for everyday, informal purposes, and this may have led, for a time, to some degree of bidialectalism. Recent research in the United States, however, has suggested that true bidialectalism is extremely rare, that speakers who acquire full control over the standard language do not retain full control over their native variety. And this would seem to be to a large extent true of communities as well as individuals; that is, as Standard English has gained ground dialect English has lost. Perhaps the situation which emerged is better described, therefore, as one in which individuals extended their stylistic repertoire to include Standard English for some uses, and dialect English for others, with the possibility of a range of mixed styles in between. As far as the community as a whole is concerned the result is a continuum running from regional dialect at one end to Standard English at the other, with individual repertoires tending more and more to cluster at the standard end. But, however that may be, it remains clear that Standard English is basically a written form of the language, neutral with regard to accent. It is impossible, for instance, to deduce the pronunciation of the present writers from what they write.

Since variation is an essential property of all human language, Standard English itself varies. It is a safe assumption, for example, that no two

Standard English speakers use exactly the same vocabulary. Nor are the differences confined to vocabulary. Americans have 'meet up with' where British speakers prefer 'meet' ('We'll meet (up with) you later'); and US speakers use 'gotten' as the past participle of 'get' in many contexts where British speakers have 'got' ('Things have gotten/got more complex lately'). Nevertheless, neither the vocabulary nor the grammar of the present paragraph will present any difficulty whatsoever to literate speakers of English, wherever they come from, and no educated speaker will fail to recognise that the paragraph is written in Standard English and not some kind of regional dialect. In short, therefore, though enormous theoretical difficulties arise if we attempt to define it, educated speakers of English have access to a kind of English which, as distinct from dialect English, enables them to communicate freely with all other educated speakers of the language.

By the time emigration from Britain began on a substantial scale in the seventeenth century, Standard English was firmly established as the vehicle for a rich and extensive literature. Above all, it was the language of the Bible. For the emigrants, accordingly, Standard English was the form of English through which they had access to their cultural and religious roots. So it continued to enjoy the high prestige it had in Britain, and with the same effect that it encouraged the adaptation of the grammar and vocabulary of writing to the spoken language, through the agency of schools and literature. Far from the dialect English in the various overseas territories separating from one another and from the dialect English of the mother country, they have remained part of one large continuum, all of them related to a standard language which is identical with none of them. Pidgins and creoles are a different matter, and these will be discussed in the next chapter.

The reality of regional dialect English, then, is continuous change, from place to place, even from person to person. In some places, particularly where some geographical feature has caused actual physical separation, differences become more numerous than elsewhere, but nowhere is the essential continuity of the language seriously interrupted, so that the boundary drawn round a regional dialect is an artificial one, in the sense that there will be both differences contained within it and similarities shared across it. This dialect continuum is manifest only in speech.

Alongside it exists the standard language, originally a local variety but now independent of any particular region. This standard, even today, is the mother tongue of only a minority of English speakers. The rest have to acquire it through the written medium and the school. Once acquired, however, it is available for both speech and writing; though we must emphasise once again that it has no standard pronunciation.

Complex as this picture may appear, it is only a partial account of dialect variation since it does not include the very important factor of social class which we have still to consider and which introduces a third dimension into the two-dimensional picture of variation we have been considering so far. At any given locality on the regional dialect continuum, we should expect to find class differences between people which manifest themselves in the way they speak.

Class, in the present context, is a socio-economic variable which relates to such more or less objectively identifiable indices as occupation, income and type of housing. In its influence on language, however, it may in addition involve such seemingly linguistically irrelevant considerations as religion and race. In Northern Ireland, for example, an individual's place on the class scale is at least partly determined by whether he is Catholic or Protestant, with the former being generally regarded as socially inferior to the latter; other things being equal. The class differences thus established correspond to dialect differences to such an extent that, especially at the lower end of the social scale, members of the two communities are able to recognise their co-religionists purely by their language. Thus, working-class Catholics and Protestants alike would recognise, for instance, 'backy', 'bardicks', 'bracky', 'brosny', 'drachy', and even 'Catholic' itself as being Catholic terms, the Protestant equivalents being 'lame', (small) 'possessions', 'speckled' (of a hen), 'small sticks', 'tedious' and 'Tague' respectively. The social effect of race can be even more distinctive; in the United States, for example, where in many cities black people constitute a separate social class whose language qualifies for the distinctive name of 'Black English'.

Class, as a linguistic factor, is discernible in both town and country, though its effect is undoubtedly a great deal more complex in the former where density of population and diversity of social interaction combine to produce what is in effect a continuum of social differentiation. It is possible, and it may for purposes of study be desirable, to divide this continuum up arbitrarily into a relatively small number of discrete classes, but the fact that this is possible should not obscure the underlying reality: that the class variable is a continuous scale and not a series of watertight compartments.

Furthermore, the linguistic variation which corresponds to this social differentiation is itself continuous. There are, in other words, no class dialects any more than there are regional dialects. It is popular in both dimensions to use (linguistically) arbitrary criteria – on the one hand geography, on the other income and similar indices. These make it possible to identify particular groups, whose speech may then be described as the dialects of those groups. But the reality is that in no case is the language of any given group either homogeneous internally, or discontinuous with contiguous varieties.

Research into socially determined language variation has suggested, in fact, that it is probably most accurately described in terms of statistical frequency of individual items, rather than in terms of class dialects. For instance, Trudgill's study conducted in Norwich into the omission of final -s as a marker of third singular in the present tense of verbs, which we earlier noted as a feature of dialect English in East Anglia, revealed the following frequencies in casual speech (1974, p. 44).

Middle Class:	middle	0%
	lower	2%
Working Class:	upper	70%
	middle	87%
	lower	97%

In other words, the higher individuals are on the social ladder, the less likely they are to omit the final -s; but, at least from the lower middle class down, occurrence is only more or less probable but never certain.

Other features yield other frequencies. Thus, the same Norwich study investigated the percentage occurrences of (a) 'n'' instead of 'ng' in, for example, 'walking', 'eating', etc., (b) glottal stops instead of 't' in, for example, 'butter', 'fatter', etc., and (c) dropped initial 'h' in, for example, 'hot', 'hammer', etc. The figures obtained (ibid., p. 48) were as follows:

		(a)	(b)	(c)
Middle Class:	middle	31	41	6
	lower	42	62	14
Working Class:	upper	87	89	40
	middle	95	92	59
	lower	100	94	61

Similar studies elsewhere, both before and since, have produced a similar picture of statistical, rather than absolute, differences of occurrence. A survey of the omission of third singular, present tense, final -s, in Detroit, where this is a dialect feature as it is in East Anglia, produced, for example, frequencies ranging from 1 per cent in upper middle-class speech to 71 per cent in lower working-class speech. In New York, Labov's experiment to determine the incidence of /r/ following a vowel, e.g. in 'car', 'tired', etc., found that in 38 per cent of instances produced by assistants in a higher-class department store /r/ was not pronounced in this position, whereas the figures for a medium-class store and a lower-class store were 49 and 83 per cent respectively.

Frequency studies of class dialect are relatively recent in origin, and work on class dialect has been in any case much less popular than regional dialect studies; figures are, accordingly, available for only a small number of features, in very few places. Moreover, since pronunciation lends itself more readily to this kind of investigation than grammar (particularly syntax) and vocabulary, it is pronunciation features which have been most quantified. There can be no doubt, however, that the pattern revealed is a general one, and we may expect to find grammatical and vocabulary differences distributed in the same fashion.

Thus, it would probably call for a good deal of ingenuity to construct a practical experimental situation which would make it possible to quantify occurrences of, to give but a few examples out of innumerable possibilities, 'She were just sat there' instead of 'She was just sitting there' in Yorkshire; 'What like was she?' in southern Scotland; 'There's happy now' against 'We're content now' in Wales; 'Is it looking for a fight, you are?' against 'Are you looking for a fight?' in Ireland; or 'ain't' against 'isn't' in North America. Nevertheless, if some convincing way could be found to quantify the occurrence of grammatical differences such as these, there is little doubt that they would be distributed in terms of more or less probability against the social class continuum rather than in distinct class dialects.

Similarly, we should expect the distribution of individual vocabulary items in relation to the social scale to be a matter of statistical frequency rather than absolute necessity at any given point on the scale. Furthermore, relative frequencies would undoubtedly vary from item to item. One would not, therefore, anticipate the same social distribution for dialect items such as, for example, 'our kid', 'daft', 'boyo', 'poorly', 'bairn', 'snicket' (a narrow passage between houses), any more than one would expect to find the same regional distribution for them.

Language variation in the social dimension, then, is essentially similar in nature to regional variation. At one end of the social scale in any given locality the most likely form of English is local dialect English, at the other end is Standard English, with, in between, grammar, vocabulary and accent varying continuously. Spoken English, therefore, has to be perceived as a three-dimensional continuum, within which it is not possible, except arbitrarily and artificially, to identify 'dialects'. It is for this reason that we have not written of 'dialects', but of 'dialect' (singular); by which we have intended to identify that kind of English which is essentially spoken, in contrast with 'Standard' English, which, as we pointed out earlier, is primarily a written form of the language.

Being primarily written, Standard English is not associated with any particular accent. In the social dimension, therefore, what usually happens with regard to accent is that variation up the social scale is in the direction of the locally prestigious pronunciation, so that educated speakers in Yorkshire, let us say, or southern Scotland, or New England, or western Australia, regularly speak Standard English with an accent which is recognisably a modified version of that in which the dialect English of the locality is spoken. In Britain, however, there also occurs a non-local accent which is sometimes used with Standard English, though never with dialect English (except, perhaps, for Eliza Doolittle's). This accent is known to phoneticians as 'RP'. The initials originally stood for 'Received Pronunciation', but the term 'Received' in this context is now, at best meaningless, even possibly misleading, and so it is better to stick to the initials.

It is important to realise that RP is not a standard pronunciation; there is, in fact, no such standard. Nor is this accent linguistically superior to other accents. Indeed, if anything it is less easy for foreigners to understand or acquire than certain local accents. Moreover, contrary to popular belief, it does vary between speakers.

But RP does have social prestige. It developed during the nineteenth century in the public schools and in the older universities and, hence, among the British ruling class. The members of that class enjoyed greater prestige in Victorian times than is now the case, and their accent, like much else about their behaviour, became associated with that prestige. So much so, indeed, that until relatively recently anybody from lower down the social scale who sought to rise to the top, or give the impression of having reached the top, usually found it at least desirable to acquire this accent. And even today, whatever may sometimes be said to the contrary, an RP accent is unquestionably an enormous asset in many spheres, especially in England.

In this chapter we have been considering the nature of dialect English. We have seen that this kind of English is characteristically spoken and that its grammar, vocabulary and pronunciation vary from place to place and also along the social scale. Dialect English, therefore, must not be perceived in terms of a set of small mini-languages which all differ from one another and from some central, 'correct' form of English, but instead as a continuum of variety in three dimensions. Standard English, itself subject to some degree of variation, is the form which is codified for teaching in schools, where it is also encouraged for use in speech. There is, however, no standard accent of English, though there is a regionally neutral class accent which enjoys considerable social prestige.

Additional Reading

Aitchison, J. (1981), *Language Change: Progress or Decay?* (London: Fontana).

Bolinger, D. L. (1957), *Interrogative Structures of American English* (Alabama: University of Alabama Press).

Brook, G. L. (1965), *English Dialects*, 2nd edn (London: André Deutsch).

Brook, G. L. (1979), *Varieties of English*, 2nd edn (London: Macmillan).

Bryant, M. M. (1962), *Current American Usage* (New York: Funk & Wagnall).

Dabke, R. (1976), *Morphology of Australian English* (Munich: Wilhelm Funk).

Dillard, J. L. (1972), *Black English* (New York: Random House).

Giles, H. (1971), 'Our reactions to accent', *New Society*, vol. 18, No. 472, pp. 713–15.

Hughes, A. and Trudgill, P. (1979), *English Accents and Dialects* (London: Edward Arnold).

Labov, W. (1966), *The Social Stratification of English in New York City* (Washington, D.C.: Center for Applied Linguistics).

Laing, M. (ed.) (1989), *Middle English Dialectology* (Aberdeen: Aberdeen University Press).

McIntosh, A. (1961), *An Introduction to the Study of Scottish Dialect* (Edinburgh: Nelson).

McIntosh, A., Samuels, M. L. and Benskin, M. (1986), *A Linguistic Atlas of Late Medieval English*, Vol. 1 (Aberdeen: Aberdeen University Press).

Malmstrom, J. and Ashley, A. (1963), *Dialects U.S.A.* (Champaign, Ill.: N.C.T.E.).

Mather, J. Y. and Speitel, H. H. (1975, 1977), *The Linguistic Atlas of Scotland*, Vols 1 & 2 (London: Croom Helm).

Milroy, J. and Milroy, L. (1985), *Authority in Language: Investigating Language Prescription and Standardization* (London: Routledge & Kegan Paul).

O'Connor, J. D. (1976), *Phonetics* (Harmondsworth: Penguin).

Orton, H. (1962), *The Survey of English Dialects; Introduction* (London: Edward Arnold).

Orton, H. and Wright, N. (1974), *A Word Geography of England* (London & New York: Seminar Press).

Pride, J. B. and Holmes, J. (eds) (1972), *Sociolinguistics* (Harmondsworth: Penguin).

Ross, A. S. C. (1954), 'Linguistic class-indicators in present-day English', *Neuphilologische Mitteilungen*, pp. 20–56.

Samuels, M. (1974), *Linguistic Evolution* (Cambridge: C.U.P.).

Todd, L. (1990), *Words Apart: A Dictionary of Northern Ireland English* (Gerrards Cross: Colin Smythe).

Trudgill, P. (1974), *Sociolinguistics* (Harmondsworth: Penguin).

Trudgill, P. (1974), *The Social Differentiation of English in Norwich* (Cambridge: C.U.P.).

Trudgill, P. (ed.) (1978), *Sociolinguistic Patterns in British English* (London: Edward Arnold).

Trudgill, P. (1983), *On Dialect* (Oxford: Blackwell).

Trudgill, P. (1984), *Language in the British Isles* (Cambridge: C.U.P.).

Turner, G. W. (1966), *The English Language in Australia and New Zealand* (London: Longmans).

Wakelin, M. (1977), *English Dialects: An Introduction*, revised edn (London: Athlone Press).

Wells, J. C. (1982), *Accents of English*, 3 vols (Cambridge: C.U.P.).

Williamson, J. V. and Burke, V. M. (1971), *A Various Language: Perspectives on American Dialects* (New York: Holt, Rinehart & Winston).

3 Pidgins and Creoles

We should now like to turn our attention to the phenomenon of pidgins and creoles, concerning which there are probably even more differences of opinion, confusions and uncertainties than with dialects.

Pidgins and creoles were at one time defined and, consequently, dismissed as 'marginal languages'. Recently, however, they have assumed a more central position in linguistics. They are being used, for example, to check theories concerning language change because their very existence challenges two related and widely held views: that the radical restructuring of languages is rare, and that change in language tends to be slow, gradual, almost imperceptible. (See Morris Swadesh's *The Origin and Diversification of Language* for a statement of such views.)

It is not easy to offer comprehensive or completely satisfactory definitions of pidgins and creoles. Just as the umbrella title 'Indo-European' comprehends a variety of languages as different as English and Hindi, Swedish and Greek, so too there are a number of distinguishable types of pidgin and creole languages. It may be useful, however, to begin with definitions which will subsequently be refined.

Pidginisation may be described as the simplification processes which result from contacts between people who speak different languages. It is perhaps worth emphasising the point that the concept of 'standard' languages and communication by means of such standards is unknown in large areas of the world today and was even more of a rarity in the past. In many such areas, contact between speakers of different languages involves and involved the emergence and exploitation of linguistic common denominators. Pidginisation is not, therefore, an unusual or altogether exotic process. It occurs in even casual contacts between people who have simple communication needs and who have little or no knowledge of each other's language.

If such contacts cease to be casual and sporadic, then pidgins frequently develop. A *pidgin* is an auxiliary language which arises to fulfil certain limited communication needs among people who have no common language. In early stages of contact, communication is often restricted to trading transactions where a detailed exchange of ideas is not required and where a relatively small vocabulary, drawn almost exclusively from the language of the dominant group, suffices. The syntactic structure of such a stage in a pidgin's development is less complex and less flexible than the structures of any of the languages involved in the contact.

It is necessary as well as useful to distinguish between two types of pidgin, the first of which may be called 'marginal'. This type of pidgin arises when speakers of two languages come into superficial contact. Such a pidgin serves limited communication needs and tends to disappear when the contact which gave rise to it is withdrawn. Such a minimal pidgin often develops between expatriates and African house-servants in West Africa and it differs markedly in form, range and flexibility from the pidgin used by house-servants to each other or to other Africans who speak different mother tongues. Korean, Vietnamese and Thai Pidgin Englishes are other examples. These latter forms of English gained currency among a limited number of Asians and Americans during the American involvement in the Far East, but they are already disappearing except in ports and in areas frequented by tourists.

Clearly distinguishable from this type of marginal language is what we may call an 'expanded' pidgin. This is one which develops in a multilingual area, which proves extremely useful in intergroup communication and which, because of its usefulness, is expanded and used outside the sphere of its origin. Almost all the West African varieties of pidgin English are of this type. They were expanded less in black-to-white than in black-to-black contact. Tok Pisin, the English-based *lingua franca* of Papua New Guinea, is another expanded pidgin. It is now used more frequently in inter-ethnic communication than any other language. Expanded pidgins differ from marginal pidgins in that one sees in them the emergence of new languages, languages with the potential to grow and spread or to disappear if their usefulness as a means of communication diminishes. It should be emphasised, however, that if expanded pidgins die they do so for sociological reasons rather than because of any linguistic deficiency.

A *creole* is a pidgin which has become the mother tongue of the members of a speech community. Often the simple structure that characterises pidgins is found also in creoles, but a creole, being a mother tongue, usually the only mother tongue of its speech community, has become capable of expressing the entire range of human experience. Its vocabulary is thus often more comprehensive, and its syntactic system more flexible and precise than the majority of even expanded pidgins, because these latter are normally used together with one or more vernacular languages. The difference between a creole like Krio, which is the only mother tongue of many Sierra Leoneans, and an expanded pidgin such as Kamtok in Cameroon, which is increasingly becoming one of the mother tongues. acquired by Cameroonians, is more readily defined in theory than in practice. In many areas of the world, including Sierra Leone, one and the same form of English may be a creole for some, a pidgin for others and a second language for the many who learn it as thoroughly as they can and certainly without, necessarily, re-pidginising it. Perhaps the clearest distinction between a creole and any pidgin is a social one. With creole speakers one can point out that at some period in the past the natural transmission of a mother tongue from one generation of speakers to the next was disrupted.

Languages which have been pidginised or creolised have almost certainly developed in every age where people have made linguistic contact with speakers of other languages. Today, examples of such languages are to be found throughout the world, in multilingual areas and along trade routes. Romaine (1988, pp. 318–22) cites 127 attested cases of languages which have undergone a form of pidginisation and that number is steadily being increased as more language contact situations are explored. More interesting, perhaps, than the mere number of pidgins and creoles being found is the fact that many of them owe nothing to the colonial expansion of European nations, although this was responsible for triggering off the majority of pidgin and creole languages which are lexically related to Indo-European languages. Indigenous lingua francas have also developed in each multilingual region. We can mention, for example, Swahili in East and Fanagalo in South Africa, Russenorsk in Europe, Urdu in the Indian sub-continent, Bahasa Malay in Asia, Hiri Motu in Papua New Guinea, Lingua Geral in South America and the so-called Chinook Jargon of North America, which almost certainly pre-dated the coming of the French and English who modified its vocabulary. All of these lingua francas share structural features with other pidgin languages, but they have the additional sociolinguistic relevance of being modifications of indigenous mother tongues which have been utilised to facilitate communication between different language groups.

So far we have looked only at modern examples of pidgins and creoles, but it seems clear that the linguistic processes which result in the emergence of such languages were also at work in the past. It is likely that a simplified form of Latin was used in the Roman army and that Latin fused with European vernaculars, developing into today's Romance languages. Similar statements can probably be made with regard to most other linguistic products of territorial or religious expansion. Arabic, Greek and English can all be examined in terms of spread, followed by divergence from the literary norm, followed by the restraining influence of the norm. It certainly seems to be true that in all widely spread empires which had a prestigious language norm, this norm, so long as it remained prestigious, tended to be superimposed on the pidginised language of early contacts and thus, for a time at least, it prevented divergences becoming so great as to impede inter-intelligibility.

Admittedly, the above suggestion is hypothetical, and the further we go from modern times and written norms, the more speculative our argument becomes, but we can leave the realm of hypothesis for attested fact when we encounter *Sabir*, the mediaeval pidgin used by the Crusaders and the

Muslims in their contacts and known also as Lingua Franca. This is the earliest attested auxiliary language and it was so widely used that samples of it can be cited from many areas of the Mediterranean. Indeed, seventeenth-century seamen like Barbot advised travellers, especially those going to Guinea and the 'American islands' that 'it is requisite for the person that designs to travel into those parts to learn languages, as English, French, Low Dutch, Portuguese and Lingua Franca' (J. and A. Churchill, 1746, p. 11). And the fact that Lingua Franca was still widely known in the eighteenth century is underlined by Swift's causing Gulliver to say (1726, p. 25):

> There were several of his priests and lawyers present (as I conjectured by their habits) who were commanded to address themselves to me, and I spoke to them in as many languages as I had the least smattering of, which were High and Low Dutch, Latin, French, Spanish, Italian and Lingua Franca; but all to no avail.

A dictionary of the Moroccan variety of Lingua Franca was published as recently as 1830 and, according to Hancock (1974, p. 2), a surprisingly large number of Lingua Franca terms have found their way into the slang vocabulary of subgroups in British and US society.

If we look more closely at English now, it is quite clear that pidginised varieties have been in existence since the sixteenth century. Literary records are usually more suggestive than accurate, yet in Marlowe's depiction of Barabas's speech in Act 4 of *The Jew of Malta* we find:

be no in tune yet: so, now, now all be in.

Two, three, four month, madam.

Very mush: monsieur, you no be his man?

me be no well

Here we can recognise such pidgin features as the use of the base form of the verb, here 'be', irrespective of the number or person of the subject; use of the singular noun form; modification of sounds; and the use of 'me' as a subject pronoun. And Defoe's *Colonel Jacque* (1722, esp. pp. 131–50) makes extensive use of a form of English that is supposedly representative of Virginian Pidgin English. The above are the earliest literary examples of pidginised English but it seems reasonable, too, to suggest that many of the changes which occurred in the language within England between the ninth and the fourteenth centuries can also be explained in terms of the pidginisation processes common to contact situations.

The knowledge we have of Old and Early Middle English dialects derives from literary texts and it is impossible to say how closely such texts reflected the speech of the people. It is not uncommon to represent the pre-Conquest language situation in England as consisting of four distinct dialects, namely, Northumbrian, Mercian, West Saxon and Kentish. It should be clear from our discussion of modern English dialects, however, that there were no discrete cut-offs between adjacent dialect areas. One variety must have merged imperceptibly into another. The literary dialects on the basis of which the four linguistic areas are postulated were clearly differentiated but the speech of the actual communities would certainly have been both internally diverse and externally continuous, as is the case today.

Increasingly, from the ninth century onwards, the Vikings invaded and settled in Britain and increasingly too, from that time, Old English changed. Wherever linguistic contact occurs, some degree of adjustment takes place, but the type of adjustment depends on the extent of the differences between the language systems of the people in contact. If the speakers use mutually intelligible dialects, the adjustments may be minimal, whereas, if the languages are very different, then the linguistic modifications may be more extreme. The speech of the Vikings was almost certainly inter-intelligible with the speech of the English because their two languages were closely related. Indeed, so close was the core vocabulary of both sets of speakers that it is not always possible to say whether a word derives from an OE or a Scandinavian dialect.

The Scandinavian influence was originally most apparent in northern and eastern dialects of OE but the influence eventually extended, at least to some extent, to all English dialects including the south-eastern dialect which was to become the nucleus of the standard language; and the influence permeated all levels of the language. Words, often pertaining to daily life, such as 'egg', 'get', 'give', 'kid', 'scrub', 'skin', 'skirt' and 'sky', were absorbed into English. The closeness of the contact is suggested by the fact that such basic function words as 'are', 'both', 'their', 'them', 'they', 'till' and 'though' were originally Scandinavian.

What is even more striking in terms of pidginisation than the absorption of Scandinavian vocabulary is the effect the Viking, and later the Norman, contact had on the structure of OE. Simplifying somewhat, one can say that early OE was a fairly highly inflected language whereas all modern dialects of English show little inflection. The word order in modern varieties of English is more rigid than it was in OE because it is mainly word order and prepositional usage which indicate the modern relationship between the words in a sentence. The juxtaposition of an OE text (A) with its modern standard equivalent (B) shows the extent of the changes OE has undergone. In addition, we offer a third version, (C), in Cameroon Kamtok to suggest that the processes by which modern English developed from OE do not differ fundamentally from those by which Kamtok developed from English.

(A) *Oft him anhaga*   *are gebideth,*
    Metudes miltse,   *theah the he modcearig*
    geond lagulade,   *longe sceolde*
    hreran mid hondum   *hrimcealde sae,*
    wadan wraeclastas: *wyrd bith ful araed.*

(B) Often the solitary man   prays to him for favour,
    For God's mercy,   although he sad at heart
    Through waterways,   must for a long time
    Stir with his hands
    (i.e. row over) the rime-cold sea,
    Traversing the paths of exile:
    fate is quite inexorable.

(C) *Plenti taim waka man tɔk fɔ i as i fɔ helep*
    Fɔ gud ting fɔ gɔd, iven wen i di taia fɔ i bele
    (i get fɔ go) fɔ ples we wata de, an fɔ lɔng, lɔng taim i get fɔ
    Muf wit i han di si we i kol pas mak,
    (i get fɔ) waka i wan fɔ dis graun: laif de dasɔ.

In particular, we should like to draw attention to the fact that (A) has two prepositions, '*geond*' and '*mid*', (B) has eight, 'to', 'for' (three times), 'at', 'through' and 'with', while (C) has nine, '*fɔ*' (eight times as a preposition) and '*wit*'. Thus, it can be seen that the function of the prepositions occurring in (B) and (C) is borne mainly by case endings in (A).

The Viking invasions appear to have initiated or at least given impetus to the simplifying and discarding of inflectional endings in OE dialects, because the beginning of their decline is already apparent before the Norman Conquest. The reason for the simplification of inflection seems clear. Scandinavian inflectional endings differed from OE ones and there was almost certainly considerable inflectional variation within the sub-dialects of both groups. In the face of such differences it seems likely that speakers tended to rely increasingly on base forms, using word order and prepositions to make up for the loss of inflectional devices. If Britain had not sustained the Norman Conquest it is likely that the loss of inflectional endings would not have been carried so far, but the Normans, from the eleventh century onwards, added to the pressures for change and simplification. Besides encouraging the loss of inflections, the speakers of Norman French (itself a contact variety of French) were also, it would seem, largely responsible for the disappearance of grammatical gender from English over the period 1200–1350. In OE, the Scandinavian dialects and Norman French, all nouns whether animate or inanimate were marked for gender, OE and the Scandinavian dialects having a three-term system, masculine, feminine and neuter, while Norman French had a two-term system, masculine and feminine. The actual genders of particular words tended to be the same in the English and the Scandinavian dialects but were only the same by chance in Norman French. Consequently, in English, grammatical gender was gradually replaced by distinctions based on sex and animateness.

The fact that all varieties of English shed grammatical gender is clearly reminiscent of the loss of gender sustained by European languages in post-fifteenth-century colonial contacts. In mediaeval England, as in coastal Africa at a later date, contact situations encouraged the abandoning or the simplification of linguistic devices which were capable of causing difficulty or confusion. We are not arguing that Middle English was a creole, although it *may* have been one for the Normans who adopted it as a mother tongue. It is true that there was no drastic interruption in the natural transmission of language from one generation to the next, but many of the language changes which occurred are widely recognised pidginisation processes. In particular, one can show that the vocabulary was modified through the adoption of words from the prestige language; that there was considerable simplification of grammatical categories like gender; that there was widespread reduction of inflection; and that word order became more rigid.

Thus far we have looked mainly at the processes which can result in the establishment of a pidgin or creole and we have suggested that such processes are more common and more widely useful in explaining language change than has hitherto been accepted. It will be useful now to turn from the general points so far discussed to an examination of the evolution, characteristics and expansion of some modern varieties of pidginised English. We shall deal only with expanded pidgins since marginal varieties are, by definition, unstable, and we shall not distinguish further between creoles and pidgins since such distinctions as can be drawn between them tend to be social and historical rather than linguistic and, as we have seen, the same language can be a creole for some speakers and a pidgin for others.

The most widely known varieties of pidginised English are those which arose as a direct result of the slave trade, and these are found on both sides of the Atlantic, along the West African coast, in the West Indies, and in the south-eastern section of the USA. The influence of what we might call Atlantic pidginised English can also be shown in many varieties of modern Black American English.

The ancestors of these varieties of pidginised English probably came into being in the late sixteenth or early seventeenth centuries on the west coast of Africa. Initially, when the contacts between Africans and English speakers were slight and of limited duration, the emerging pidgin would have had a small vocabulary which would have been supplemented by gesture and perhaps mime. The vocabulary of such a pidgin tends to derive mainly from the language of the dominant group – English in the case of West African–English contact – but words from other languages, such as *blai* (basket), *palava* (row, debate), *pikin* (child) and *savi* (know) from Portuguese, may be incorporated, especially if they are known to both contacting groups. Such a makeshift pidgin is of limited value and only two fates are possible: it may be expanded or it may disappear. Evidence from the study of many world pidgins suggests that the former fate is confined to pidgins which arise in multilingual areas. There is no reason, however, why successive pidgins should not arise in one area, in a port, for example, each one sharing similarities with earlier varieties.

Expanded pidgins have developed in multilingual areas and it seems probable that they were expanded by the indigenous people because of their value in permitting more extensive intergroup communication than had hitherto been possible. In this early phase it seems likely that there was considerable reliance on the local languages for lexical and syntactic expansion. The reliance can be seen in several ways. First, words pertaining exclusively to local culture were borrowed. Such words can be listed from both Atlantic and Pacific varieties of pidgin English, suggesting that cultural contact between native and non-native was minimal. In Cameroon's Kamtok, for example, we find such African words as *fɔn* (chief), *fufu* (food), *kɔnggɔsa* (chat), *mimbo* (alcohol), *nchinda* (messenger of the fon) and *ngambi* (ghost, spirit), and similar sets are found in Papua New Guinea's Tok Pisin where we find *bilum* (local net), *kaikai* (eat, food), *kibung* (meeting), *lotu* (religious belief) and *tambaran* (spirits of ancestors). Secondly, and not surprisingly in view of a pidgins's role in facilitating intergroup contact, the indigenous words that were common to many languages were borrowed. *Nyam*, for example, was adopted into a number of West African pidgins meaning 'eat, food' because it was a common Bantu form and thus widely used and understood. Thirdly, we find *calques* or loan translations such as *dei klin* (<day + clean) for 'daybreak', *krai dai* (<cry + die) for 'mourn' and *was bele* (<wash + belly) meaning 'last child' in various pidginised Englishes of the Atlantic. Calques had the merit of utilising English words in the translation of local ideas, metaphors and idioms, many of which were again common to a large number of languages. It seems likely, indeed, that it is at the level of idiomatic language that pidgins which are lexically related to English can clearly show the influence of their speakers' mother tongues. For example, the words '*sɔk*' (<suck) and '*tit*' (<teeth) occur in many English-based pidgins but the expression '*sɔk tit*' meaning 'insult, disparage' as in Kamtok's '*Hu bi yu? Yu tink sei yu fit sɔk tit fɔ mi?*' (Who do you think you are? Do you think you can insult me?) would not be meaningful outside an African-influenced milieu. On the other hand, looking at the pidgin English of Papua New Guinea, Tok Pisin (<Talk Pidgin), one can point to a set of compounds involving the use of '*wan*' (<one):

wan bel	(<one belly)	–	twin
wan blut	(<one blood)	–	blood relation, kinsman
wan haus	(<one house)	–	those living in the same house

wan lain	(<one line)	–	age mate
wan pis	(<one piece)	–	orphan
wan tok	(<one talk)	–	compatriot, speaker of the same language
wan rot	(<one road)	–	fellow traveller.

All of these compounds share the feature of implied unity. In this usage, the pidgin parallels the Papua New Guinean vernaculars and differs from Standard English and from other, non-related pidgins.

The more widely used a pidgin is, the more expanded it tends to become, and two other types of vocabulary growth occur. First, there is often increased influence and pressure from the lexical source language. This is particularly apparent in the case of English pidgins where Standard English is the language of education and government of the area concerned. Words like 'vote', 'university' and 'pension' are often adopted into the pidgin, together with the modern English words for items for which the pidgin already has a form. This can be illustrated from Kamtok:

Early Pidgin	**New Borrowing**	**English**
bele	*stɔmak*	stomach
kɔmbi	*fren*	friend, companion
manhan	*rait*	right
wumanhan	*lef*	left
sabi	*no*	know

Secondly, the expanded pidgin can use its own internal resources to coin new words for concepts for which the older variety did not provide. This can be illustrated by reference to Tok Pisin where we find:

as ples	(<ass [= source] place)	place of birth
bikhangre	(<big hungry)	famine
bikskul	(<big school)	university
hambakman	(<humbug man)	flirt, loafer
kilman	(<kill man)	murderer
kukimnus	(<cook + him nose)	courtship, kiss
mausgras	(<mouth grass)	moustache
tinksave	(<think know)	intelligence

Sometimes, too, syntactic devices can be used to express nuances with a small vocabulary. Thus, in Tok Pisin, *-im* normally indicates that the verb to which it is attached is transitive and *pinis* (<finish) is an auxiliary verb which indicates that the action is finished:

Em i kikim mi (he kicks me)
Em i laikim mi (she likes me)

Em i kam pinis (he has come)
Em i go pinis (she has gone)

They can also be used now, however, to expand the vocabulary so that we find such sets as:

dai	(<die)	be unconscious
dai pinis		die
laip	(<life)	life
laipim		enliven
orait	(<all right)	all right
oraitim		fix, mend
promis	(<promise)	promise
promis pinis		keep a promise
ris	(<rich)	rich
risim		enrich

A further phase in the development of a pidgin is what has been called a 'post-creole continuum', although the phenomenon thus described is not limited to areas where pidgins have become the mother tongue of a speech community. When a creole or expanded pidgin exists in a community where its lexical source language is the language of education and politics, as is the case in the West Indies, in West Africa, in Hawaii and in Papua New Guinea, the two linguistic systems inter-influence each other with the result that one finds, not two distinct systems, but an unbroken spectrum between the pidgin or creole on the one hand and the prestigious standard language on the other. There is no point on the continuum where we find a sharp break between the sub-varieties, as is clear if we look at the following range of possibilities that can occur in the English creole continuum of Guyana in South America. For convenience of reference, however, the terms 'basilect', 'mesolect' and 'acrolect' are applied to distinguish the variants which are furthest from the standard language (basilect) from those which are closest (acrolect):

mi gii am *mi bin gii am* *mi bin gii ii* *mi bin gi ii* *mi di gi ii*	basilectal variants
mi di gi hii *a di gi ii* *a di gii ii* *a did gi ii* *a did giv ii* *a did giv hii*	mesolectal variants

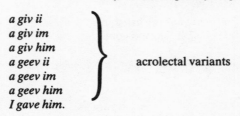

a giv ii
a giv im
a giv him
a geev ii   acrolectal variants
a geev im
a geev him
I gave him.

(The above range of possibilities open to a speaker is provided by the Guyanese scholar, George Cave, and the spelling system derives from Cassidy and LePage's *Dictionary of Jamaican English* where a doubling of letters indicates a long vowel.) A second example comes from a Kamtok narrative where the story-teller utilises *man pikin, man pikin dem, boi dem, boiz*, and *boiz dem* for 'boys':

> *So dat tri man pikin tek di bot go* . . . (So those three boys took the boat and went off . . .)
> *Di man pikin dem savi sei* . . . (The boys knew that)
> *Oke, wan dei dat boi dem kɔmɔt* . . . (Okay, one day those boys came out . . .)
> *Di boiz bin du bad an dem go luk trɔbu bad* . . . (The boys did wrong and they will suffer . . .)
> *So no man no savi wɛti hapɛn fɔ di boiz dem* . . . (So nobody knows what happened to the boys . . .)

Similar continua can be cited from many areas of the world where a non-standard variety of English coexists with the more prestigious standard language. There is, for example, considerable evidence (Holm, 1988) that Black English in the United States is an example of a creole English which has been exposed to standard and non-creole varieties for such a long time that it is now in an advanced state of decreolisation. The existence of Black English may suggest that, in the past, creoles which coexisted with their prestigious lexical source languages may have eventually merged with them, becoming indistinguishable from them. It can certainly be shown that converging processes are at work today in all areas of the world where non-standard varieties of English coexist with the standard. In Northern Ireland, for example, similar continua are found in the speech of people whose ancestral mother tongue was Gaelic. Referring to the fact that the children have eaten all the biscuits, a mother might say:

> Yiz is after atin all the biscuits on me
> Yiz iz after atin all the biscuits
> Yiz have all the biscuits ate on me
> Yiz has all the biscuits ate
> Youse have ate all the biscuits

Youse have all the biscuits ate on me
Youse have eaten all the biscuits on me
Youse have eaten all the biscuits
You've eaten all the biscuits

It is perhaps worth emphasising that the variant used is not randomly chosen but may depend on such factors as age, education, degree of intimacy, social position and religious affiliation of the speaker and the addressees. The standard sentence would not be used by a rural Catholic to members of her own family.

Continua such as those illustrated from Guyana, Cameroon and Northern Ireland are to be found, as we have suggested, wherever standard and non-standard varieties coexist. They tend to be more extensive, however, where the non-standard varieties have been influenced by other languages, by African mother tongues in the case of Guyana and Cameroon, by Gaelic in the case of Northern Ireland. We should now like to focus on some of the characteristics of pidgin languages.

The pidgins which have so far been investigated by linguists share a number of structural similarities, although no single structure is unique to them and thus capable of marking out a pidgin from other world languages.

The most immediately striking feature of pidgins is that they are syntactically simpler than the languages to which they are lexically related. Berry (1971, p. 527) expresses the matter thus:

> That inflection is the commonest casualty in the contact situation seems true of both European and African pidgins. The massive reduction of the Bantu nominal prefix system in Fanagalo and other indigenous African pidgins parallels the less striking loss of gender, case and number distinctions in European pidgins.

With regard to pidgin Englishes, such loss of inflection can be illustrated from both the Atlantic and the Pacific regions, taking Cameroon's Kamtok as an example of the former and Papua New Guinea's Tok Pisin as an example of the latter.

(1) Pidgin Englishes tend not to mark plurality in the noun:

Kamtok	English	Tok Pisin
wan pikin	a/one child	*wanpela pikinini*
tu pikin	two children	*tupela pikinini*
tri man	three men	*tripela man*
foa wuman	four women	*fopela meri*

(The examples given are taken from the most basilectal varieties. Different forms certainly occur in the continuum. In mesolectal varieties of

Kamtok, for example, we find *tri man dem* and acrolectal speakers can use *tri men (dem)*.)

(2) There is no concordial agreement between subject and predicate in the third person singular of the non-past tense:

Kamtok	English	Tok Pisin
dring di milik	drink the milk	*dring susu*
pusi dring di milik	Pussy drinks the milk	*pusi dring susu*

(3) With regard to the verb, temporal and aspectual distinctions are either understood from the context:

Kamtok	English	Tok Pisin
i kam yestadei	he came yesterday	*em i kam asde*
kam	come	*kam*

or are made overt by means of auxiliaries:

Kamtok	English	Tok Pisin
i dɔng kam	he has come	*em i kam pinis*
i bin kam	he came	*em i bin kam*
i go kam	he will come	*bai em i kam*
i savi kam	he/she comes often	*em i save kam*

When the auxiliaries co-occur, they do so in a fixed order with time preceding aspect:

Kamtok	English	Tok Pisin
a bin di tanap	I was standing	*mi bin sanap i stap*
a bin dɔng di rid	I have been reading	*mi rit pinis i stap*

(4) Questions are indicated by intonation and question words rather than by inversion or the use of 'do' as in Standard English:

Kamtok	English	Tok Pisin
yu laikam?	do you like it?	*yu laikim em?*
usai Papa dei?	where is Daddy?	*we Papa stap?*
haumoch yu get?	how much have you?	*hamas yu gat?*

(5) The negative marker precedes the first element in the verb phrase:

Kamtok	English	Tok Pisin
yu no bin siam?	did you not see it?	*yu no bin lukim em?*
dem no kam	they did not come	*ol i no kam*

and multiple negation is a common form of emphasis:

> *No man no laik mi no smɔl* (nobody likes me even a little)

(6) The rarity or non-occurrence of inflectional endings in pidgins results in words being multifunctional, that is, they can occur in more than one word class. This fact is, however, truer of Atlantic pidgins than Pacific pidgins. In Kamtok, for example, a word such as *bad* derives from the English adjective 'bad' but its class in Kamtok can only be decided when we see it in context:

dat bad pikin (that bad child)	adjective
A laikam bad (I like it a lot)	adverb
A bin du bad (I did wrong)	noun
i bad tumɔch (he is very bad)	verb

Kamtok's multifunctionality can also be shown by looking at the ways in which *waka* (<walk) differs from its English equivalent. It functions like 'walk' in:

> *i go waka fɔ haus* (he'll walk to the house/home)

but it can also be used in such non-English constructions as:

> *waka man no di kuk nkanda* (a travelling man has no time to cook tough meat)
> *a bin go waka ma sista* (I went to visit my sister).

Multifunctionality is also a feature of Tok Pisin as one might expect, in view of the fact that multifunctionality occurs in English in such words as 'right' which can be an adjective in 'the right decision', an adverb in 'do it right this time', a noun in 'right will triumph in the end' and a verb in 'you can't right every wrong'. In Tok Pisin, we find items used as both nouns and verbs:

> *em i gat amamas* (he has happiness)
> *em i amamas* (he delights)
> *em i gat sik* (he has an illness)
> *em i sik* (he is ill)

But Tok Pisin and related Pacific varieties have a regular system of affixation, whereby adjectives usually have a suffix *-pela* (<fellow), as in *bikpela man* (a big man) and *gutpela tok* (good talk). And transitive verbs are marked by the suffix *-im*, as in *em i lukim mi* (he is watching me) and *em i harim mi* (she hears me). Such affixes limit the nature and extent of the multifunctionality in Tok Pisin.

It has often been claimed that pidgins have small vocabularies. Robert A. Hall, Jr., one of the first scholars to see the value and potential of pidgins, said: 'From a structural point of view, the essential characteristic of a pidgin language is that it is sharply reduced in its pronunciation and grammar and in its vocabulary' (1966, p. 25). When compared with Standard English, it is certainly true that pidgins have small vocabularies, but two points should be borne in mind. In the first place, there are few languages whose vocabularies would not suffer when compared with Standard English and, secondly, many pidgins have techniques for vocabulary expansion which are not systematically employed in the standard language. Reduplication, for example, is quite extensively used in English-based pidgins to reduce the number of homophones:

Kamtok	English	Tok Pisin
hama	hammer	
hamahama	enormous	
	laugh	*lap*
	loincloth	*laplap*

to extend the meaning of the simple form:

Kamtok	English	Tok Pisin
ben	bend	
benben	crooked	
	mark	*mak*
	variegated	*makmak*

to imply repeated or continuous action:

Kamtok	English	Tok Pisin
tif	steal	
tiftif	steal habitually	
	think	*ting*
	reflect	*tingting*

to emphasise a quality:

Kamtok	English	Tok Pisin
big	big	
big big	very big	
	good	*gutpela*
	very good	*gutpelagutpela*

and to express the equivalent of 'one by one', 'one each':

Kamtok	English	Tok Pisin
wanwan	one by one	*wanpelawanpela*
tutu	two each	*tupelatupela.*

Standard English has many lexical sets of the type 'mare, horse, filly, foal', 'ewe, ram, lamb', with 'horse' and 'sheep' as the respective superordinate terms. In such sets the semantic relationships are not indicated by the forms. In pidgins, such sets do not occur, but the means of expressing the same distinctions do. A base form which is unmarked for gender or number is adopted and such a form is used with the words for 'man', 'woman' and 'child' to establish lexical sets where the relationships are overt:

Kamtok	English	Tok Pisin
pig	pig	*pik*
man pig	boar	*pik man*
wuman pig	sow	*pik meri*
man pikin pig	piglet (male)	*pik pikinini man*
wuman pikin pig	piglet (female)	*pik pikinini meri*

Nevertheless, in spite of the ability which an expanded pidgin possesses to increase its vocabulary in response to social or technological changes, pidgins are by definition no one's mother tongue. It is not, therefore, surprising that lexical gaps occur in certain fields. Kamtok, for example, has a well-developed liturgical vocabulary because of its use by missionaries:

Ma brɔda dem, mek una lukɔt fɔ dat kain fashɔn wei una gɛtam. Mek una waka laik sɛns pipul, an no bi laik fulish pipul. Mek una lukɔt fain, fɔseka wi dei fɔ bad taim. Mek una no bi laik fulish pipul, bɔt mek una trai fɔ savi di ting wei God i wan. Mek una no fulop una bele wit mimbo wei i di spoil man i laif . . . (St Paul's Epistle to the Ephesians, 5: 15–18).

It is limited, however, when compared with the indigenous languages in the semantic fields of kinship, hunting and farming. Indeed, animal names are very inadequately covered in Kamtok, the most widely used terms being '*bif*' meaning 'animal' and '*bush bif*' meaning 'wild animal'. Perhaps these lexical gaps are not surprising in view of the fact that cultural activities tend to be confined to groups that share a mother tongue and so there is much less need for a pidgin in such spheres. Similar lexical lacunae can also be cited from Tok Pisin where, according to Mühlhaüsler (1975, p. 7), the gaps most apparent include 'traditional religion, modern technology, natural history' and he notes that there is also a 'peculiar lack of names for smaller animals and plants, and a shortage of descriptive adjectives'.

Closely allied to the paucity of vocabulary in certain semantic domains we have another characteristic of pidgins, a reduction in language functions. Drawing attention to this characteristic of pidgins, Samarin (in Hymes, 1971, p. 126) had this to say:

> Pidginisation should be seen as *any consistent reduction of the functions of language both in its grammar and its use*. The key word here is 'functions'. With regard to the various uses to which language is put, this characterisation means that a language is used to talk about less topics, or in fewer contexts, to indicate fewer social relations. Imagine the whole gamut of uses to which any specific language is put, and a pidginised form of that language would have fewer such uses.

It would be foolish to underrate the functional reduction which is a marker of most pidgins, even the expanded ones, but it would be grossly inaccurate to suggest that creoles suffer from the same inadequacies. Creoles are mother tongues and are capable of fulfilling all linguistic functions. It must not be forgotten that Atlantic creoles have been used for centuries for all normal language activities including the transmission of oral traditions and folk beliefs.

We have suggested that pidginisation is a natural, perhaps unavoidable, consequence of contact between communities, especially non-literate communities; that expanded pidgins develop in multilingual communities where their usefulness in facilitating inter-ethnic contact is exploited; that pidgins, however expanded, may be used for fewer purposes than mother tongue languages but that the same limitation need not apply to creoles although they, like the majority of world languages, are infrequently used in formal education; and that many world languages including English and French may have developed from creoles. This last point allows us to stress the fact that the social stigma attached to many modern creoles is not to be ascribed to any linguistic deficiency. But many questions still remain unanswered, questions such as: why did pidgins arise? why is a standard language or established dialect not acquired? why do apparently unrelated pidgins and creoles have so many structural affinities? These questions cannot be answered in full because they merge into the larger questions which continue to tease linguists: why do languages change? are there linguistic universals, features which are common to all languages, features which are more clearly discernible in pidgins or in recently creolised languages?

Theories have been advanced in an attempt to answer the questions relating to pidgins and creoles. They have been compared to 'baby-talk' versions of languages and to nautical common-denominator language varieties which crystallised on ships because of the heterogeneous nature of crews and were then spread along trade routes. It has been argued that pidgins and creoles are similar because, fundamentally, languages are similar and simplification processes are similar and common to all speech communities. Such theories have only provided partial answers to the linguistic problems posed by the existence of pidgins and creoles and have stressed the similarity of all languages, pidginised or not.

But the recent detailed examination of pidgins has suggested that they might be extremely valuable to linguists in their search for linguistic universals because, in these languages, we find basic, unselfconscious communication. Putting the matter somewhat simplistically one might say that the linguists who probe into non-surface levels of standard languages produce increasingly more abstract 'deep structure' features because it is by no means easy to isolate features which may well depend on how the human mind is structured. One way of discovering linguistic universals is to follow the American lead and probe, ever more deeply, into standard, idealised English. Another method, and one which might offer additional possibilities of success, is to analyse the forms of language used by non-literate multilinguals. It is surely not an accident that in areas like multilingual West Africa, and in multilingual Austronesian communities in Papua New Guinea, areas where pidginisation is endemic, it is not only the pidgins which share structural features but the vernacular mother tongues as well. Perhaps in the speech patterns of multilingual individuals, not influenced by prescriptivism, one finds clues to the deep structure of all languages, clues to the way people structure both language and experience.

A great deal of work has been done on pidgins and creoles in the past twenty years and although there is still much to be done, we now know that stable, pidginised languages have their own systematic patterning, their own logic, their own potential and their own value as viable communication systems. But, beyond this, they have become of central importance in the developing science of linguistics, in that they are providing valuable clues towards the understanding of what Language is and what features may exist in the biological blueprints of all language-using people.

Additional Reading

Achebe, C. (1960), *No Longer at Ease* (London: Heinemann).

Achebe, C. (1972), *Girls at War* (London: Heinemann).

Achebe, C. (1987), *Anthills of the Savanna* (London: Heinemann).

Adams, R. (1974), *Watership Down* (Harmondsworth: Penguin).

Aig-Imoukhuede, F. (1982), *Pidgin Stew and Sufferhead* (Ibadan: Heinemann Educational Books).

Alleyne, M. C. (1980), *Comparative Afro-American: An Historical Comparative Study of English-based Afro-American Dialects of the New World* (Ann Arbor: Karoma Publishing, Inc.).

Andersen, R. (ed.) (1981), *New Dimensions in Second Language Acquisition Research* (Rowley, Mass.: Newbury House).

Andersen, R. (ed.) (1983), *Pidginization and Creolization as Language Acquisition* (Rowley: Newbury House).

Anderson, J. M. (1973), *Structural Aspects of Language Change* (London: Longman).

Bailey, B. L. (1966), *Jamaican Creole Syntax* (Cambridge: Cambridge University Press).

Baker, P. (1972), *Kreol: A Description of Mauritian Creole* (London: C. Hurst).

Baker, P. and Corne, C. (1980), *Isle de France Creole* (Ann Arbor: Karoma Publishers, Inc.).

Berry, J. (1971), 'Pidgins and Creoles in Africa', *Current Trends in Linguistics, 7* (The Hague: Mouton), pp. 510–36.

Bickerton, D. (1981), *Roots of Language* (Ann Arbor: Karoma Publishers, Inc.).

Bickerton, D. (1986), 'Beyond Roots: the five-year test'. Paper presented at the Winter meeting of the Linguistic Society of America, Baltimore.

Bloomfield, L. (1933), *Language* (London: Allen and Unwin).

Brown, R. (1973), *A First Language* (Cambridge, Mass.: Harvard University Press).

Carr, E. B. (1972), *Da Kine Talk: From Pidgin to Standard English in Hawaii* (Honolulu: Hawaii University Press).

Cassidy, F. G. (1971), *Jamaica Talk: Three Hundred Years of the English Language in Jamaica* (London: Macmillan).

Cassidy, F. G. and LePage, R. B. (1980), *Dictionary of Jamaican English* (Cambridge: Cambridge University Press).

Chaudenson, R. (1979), *Les Créoles Français* (Évreux: Nathan).

Churchill, J. and A. (1744–76), *A Collection of Voyages and Travels* (London: Henry Linton and John Osborn).

Churchill, W. (1911), *Beach-la-Mar* (Washington: Carnegie Institution, no. 164).

Comrie, B. (1981), *Language Universals and Linguistic Typology* (Oxford: Blackwell).

Corne, C. (1977), *Seychelles Creole Grammar: Elements for Indian Ocean Proto-Creole Reconstruction* (Tübingen: Gunter Narr).

Dalphinis, M. (1985), *Caribbean and African Languages: Social History, Language, Literature and Education* (London: Karia Press).

DeCamp, D. and Hancock, I. F. (eds) (1974), *Pidgins and Creoles: Current Trends and Prospects* (Washington: Georgetown University Press).

Dillard, J. L. (1972), *Black English* (New York: Random House).

Dillard, J. L. (1975), *Perspectives on Black English* (The Hague: Mouton).

Dutton, T. E. (1973), *Conversational New Guinea Pidgin* (Canberra: Pacific Linguistics, D-12).

Dutton, T. E. and Kakare, I. (1977), *The Hiri Trading Language of Central Papua: A First Survey* (Waigani, Papua New Guinea: Occasional Paper 15).

Edwards, V. (1979), *The West Indian Language Issue in British Schools* (London: Routledge and Kegan Paul).

Ferguson, C. A. (1971), 'Absence of copula and the Notion of Simplicity: a Study of Normal Speech, Baby Talk, Foreigner Talk and Pidgins', in Dell Hymes, *Pidginisation and Creolization of Languages*, pp. 141–50.

Ferraz, I. L. (1979), *The Creole of Sao Tomé* (Johannesburg: Witwatersrand University Press).

Fyle, C. N. and Jones, E. D. (1980), *A Krio-English Dictionary* (Oxford University Press and Sierra Leone University Press).

Germain, R. (1980), *Grammaire Créole* (Paris: L'Harmattan).

Gilbert, G. G. (ed.) (1987), *Pidgin and Creole Languages: Essays in Memory of John E. Reinecke* (Honolulu: Hawaii University Press).

Goodman, M. F. (1964), *A Comparative Study of Creole French Dialects* (The Hague: Mouton).

Hall, R. A. Jr. (1943), *Melanesian Pidgin English* (Baltimore: Linguistic Society of America).

Hall, R. A. (1944), 'Chinese Pidgin English: grammar and texts', *Journal of the American Oriental Society*, vol. 64, pp. 95–113.

Hall, R. A. (1966), *Pidgin and Creole Languages* (Ithaca: Cornell University Press).

Hancock, I. F. (1972), *A List of Place Names in the Pacific North-West derived from the Chinook Jargon with a Word-list of the Language* (Vancouver: Vancouver Public Library).

Hancock, I. F. (1973), 'Remnants of the Lingua Franca in Britain', *The University of Southern Florida Language Quarterly*, XI, 3–4, pp. 35–6.

Hancock, I. F. (1984), 'Shelta and Polari', in P. Trudgill, *Languages in Britain*, pp. 384–403.

Hancock, I. F. (1986), *Diversity and Development in English-related Creoles* (Ann Arbor: Karoma Publishing, Inc.).

Hancock, I. F. (1987), 'A preliminary classification of the anglophone Atlantic creoles, with syntactic data from thirty-three representative dialects', in G. G. Gilbert, *Pidgin and Creole Languages*, pp. 264–334.

Holm, J. (1988–89), *Pidgin and Creole Languages*, 2 vols (Cambridge: Cambridge University Press).

Hymes, Dell (ed.) (1971), *Pidginization and Creolization of Languages* (Cambridge: Cambridge University Press).

Kachru, B. B. (1982), *The Indianization of English: the English Language in India* (New Delhi: Oxford University Press).

LePage, R. L. and Tabouret-Keller, A. (1985), *Acts of Identity* (Cambridge: Cambridge University Press).

Markey, T. L. (ed. and translator) (1979), *Schuchardt* (Ann Arbor: Karoma Publishing, Inc.).

Mihalic, F. (1971), *The Jacaranda Dictionary and Grammar of Melanesian Pidgin* (Milton, Queensland: The Jacaranda Press).

Morris, M. (ed.) (1982), *Louise Bennett: Selected Poems* (Kingston, Jamaica: Sangster's Book Stores).

Mühlhaüsler, P. (1975), 'Creolisation of New Guinea Pidgin' (Canberra: mimeographed).

Mühlhaüsler, P. (1979), *Growth and Structure of the Lexicon of New Guinea Pidgin* (Canberra: Pacific Linguistics, Series C. 52).

Mühlhaüsler, P. (1986), *Pidgin and Creole Linguistics* (Oxford: Basil Blackwell).

Muysken, P. (1981), *Generative Studies on Creole Languages* (Dordrecht: Foris).

Muysken, P. and Smith, N. (eds) (1985), *Substrata versus Universals in Creole Genesis* (Amsterdam: John Benjamins).

Oyekunle, S. (1983), *Katakata for Sofahead* (London: Macmillan).

Reinecke, J. (1937), *Marginal Languages*, Ph.D. thesis, Yale.

Reinecke, J. et al. (1975), *A Bibliography of Pidgin and Creole Languages* (Honolulu: University of Hawaii Press).

Rickford, J. (1988), *Dimensions of a Creole Continuum* (Stanford: Stanford University Press).

Romaine, S. (1988), *Pidgin and Creole Languages* (London: Longman).

Samarin, W. (1967), *A Grammar of Sango* (The Hague: Mouton).

Schneider, G. D. (1966), *West African Pidgin English* (Athens, Ohio: Hartford Seminary Foundation).

Sylvain, S. (1936), *Le Créole Haitien: morphologie et syntaxe* (Port-au-Prince, Haiti: Imprimerie de Meester).

Swadesh, M. (1972), *The Origin and Diversification of Language* (London: Routledge and Kegan Paul).

Taylor, D. (1977), *Languages of the West Indies* (Baltimore: Johns Hopkins University Press).

Todd, L. (1974), 'An analysis of the BE verb in Cameroon Pidgin', *Archivum Linguisticum*, vol. 4, pp. 1–15.

Todd, L. (1979), *Some Day Been Dey: West African Pidgin Folktales* (London: Routledge and Kegan Paul).

Todd, L. (1981), *Varieties of English Around the World: Cameroon* (Heidelberg: Julius Groos Verlag).

Todd, L. (1984), *Modern Englishes: Pidgins and Creoles* (Oxford: Blackwell).

Todd, L. (1990), *Pidgins and Creoles* (London: Routledge).

Todd, L. and Hancock, I. F. (1986), *International English Usage* (London: Croom Helm).

Trudgill, P. (ed.) (1984), *Languages in Britain* (Cambridge: Cambridge University Press).

Turner, L. D. (1949), *Africanisms in the Gullah Dialect* (Chicago: Chicago University Press).

Valdman, A. (ed.) (1977), *Pidgin and Creole Linguistics* (Bloomington: Indiana University Press).

Woolford, E. and Washabaugh, W. (eds) (1983), *The Social Context of Creolization* (Ann Arbor: Karoma Publishing, Inc.).

Wurm, S. A. (ed.) (1979), *New Guinea and Neighbouring Areas: A Sociolinguistic Laboratory* (The Hague: Mouton).

Wurm, S. A. and Harris, J. (1963), *Police Motu: An Introduction to the Trade Language of Papua* (Linguistic Circle of Canberra, Series 1.1).

Wurm, S. A. and Mühlhaüsler, P. (eds) (1985), *Handbook of Tok Pisin (New Guinea Pidgin)* (Canberra: Pacific Linguistics, Series C. 70).

Young, H. (1976), *A Directory of Solomon Pidgin Idioms* (Honiara, mimeographed).

4 *Style*

In Chapter 2 we discussed that kind of variety in English which correlates with distance, whether physical or social, between individuals, and which is usually called 'dialect'. We turn now to a different kind of variety; that which we find from one situation to another in the English of one individual. This kind of personal variation we shall call 'style'.

Consider, for example, the following different ways of asking the time:

(1) Excuse me, could you tell me the right time, please?
(2) What time is it, please?
(3) What's the time?
(4) How's the enemy?
(5) Time?
(6) How much longer have we got?
(7) My watch seems to have stopped . . .

They are all correct English, in that any one of them could be used by an educated speaker of English without a qualm provided it was used in an appropriate situation. Thus (1) might be addressed to a stranger (a fellow passenger on a train, for instance), but could hardly be said by a husband to his wife. Similarly (4) might be used to a workmate, or to an acquaintance in a pub, but not, perhaps, to the vicar. Each of the above formulations would be appropriate in some situations, but inappropriate in others. Speakers who would use the same one all the time, whatever the circumstances, could not be said to have a full command of English.

Different situations, that is, call for different ways of saying the same thing. Furthermore, though many of the situations in which we may find ourselves recur regularly – such as buying a newspaper or greeting colleagues – there will be many other situations which occur seldom, but which we must nevertheless cope with. Any one of us may, for instance, be asked to give evidence in a court of law, be interviewed for a new job, or be called upon to propose a vote of thanks; perhaps from time to time or perhaps only once in a lifetime. We must all, consequently, be sensitive to the specific linguistic demands of particular situations, and flexible enough in our use of language to respond appropriately to those demands.

What we shall be discussing in the present chapter, then, is the phenomenon of stylistic variation. On the one hand, we shall be looking at language in order to ask what it is that changes from situation to situation; and, on the other, we shall be trying to identify the non-linguistic factors in situations to which the language changes correspond.

Before we embark on this discussion, there is one possible source of confusion we should like to remove. We have identified the kind of variety we wish to examine with the language of the individual, that is, with the idiolect, by which we have implied a distinction between 'dialect', as the kind of variety which is found between idiolects, and 'style', as the kind of variety found within idiolects. A number of other writers have chosen a rather different approach and have distinguished dialect, defined as 'language according to user', from what they have called 'register', defined by contrast with dialect as 'language according to use'. In other words, they have identified the second kind of variety, not with the individual speaker, but with the individual situation (see Halliday, McIntosh and Strevens; Brook; Gregory and Carroll).

The view adopted here is that the promise of precision implied by the register approach is ultimately unhelpful. In particular, the implication is to be strongly resisted that there exist discrete 'registers', or that the relationship between a given situation and the language occurring in that situation is ever close enough to enable us to identify a particular 'register'. It is true that in English, as in every other natural language, there exist strongly situation-bound language features, the recurrence of which may indicate a situation of a particular, though usually fairly general, type. The reader may in this way recognise the probable provenance of such items as 'brethren', 'Almighty God', 'the Lord', for instance, or 'my learned friend', 'the plaintiff', 'the defendant'.

While correspondences of this kind are numerous, they are, nevertheless, the exception rather than the rule. They are also both general and partial. They are general in that the occurrence of situation-bound features does not usually permit any real precision in the definition of the corresponding situation, so that discussions of register tend to be in vague, general terms; for example, Brook (1973) refers to 'the two registers of commerce and journalism'. And they are partial in that the predictable, situation-bound terms usually constitute only a relatively small part of the language used.

In such circumstances, it is misleading to imply that each situation may be objectively defined by reference to 'parameters' such as field, tenor and mode (Gregory and Carroll, 1978) and that once defined it selects its own language variety. Possibly this, and the further implication that the number of situation-types is determinate, is a consequence of the vagueness of most 'register' discussion. On the other hand, it is in our view more likely that the vagueness of discussion has itself to be explained by reference to the unsatisfactory nature of the notion of register.

The present discussion will, accordingly, look at situationally conditioned variety in language in terms of 'style' and not 'register'. The view taken here is that speakers are not to be regarded as linguistic prisoners of some objectively identifiable situation, but as the possessors of a unique store of language, from which they are able to select variably in order to achieve their own private ends in a context consisting of a complex of subjectively perceived elements. Our competence in selecting from our own unique store is, in fact, a very important facet of what we think of as *personality*. If we were always 'linguistic prisoners', then one of the chief aids others make use of in summing us up would be removed.

The individual store must not be seen as an inventory of styles, from which the speaker is able to select a style-as-a-whole appropriate to a context-as-a-whole. Rather, the style on any given occasion is the product of many separate language choices, made in response to a network of contextual factors, without, however, any one-to-one correspondence between elements of language on the one hand and elements of context on the other. Style, therefore, like dialect, should be viewed as continuous variety and not as a set of discrete varieties; and it is describable in terms of tendencies only, and not of immutable laws.

In discussing dialect variation in Chapter 2, we confined our attention to the sound system, vocabulary and grammar of English. Our discussion of style will also be concerned with these three levels, but we must now introduce an additional dimension, that of 'paralinguistic' behaviour, by which we mean the kind of communicative behaviour – such as gesture and tone of voice – which a speaker engages in while talking, and which contributes to meaning. No doubt this level of language is also subject to dialect variation, but little research has been done on it.

It must be admitted that even with regard to style relatively little is known about the paralinguistic level, and there is neither an agreed framework nor agreed terminology to facilitate discussion. But paralinguistic phenomena are an essential element of human speech, and as such cannot be overlooked. And since, as distinct from dialect variation, they represent a source of variation within the control of the individual, they are clearly more appropriately considered in the discussion on style; by definition variety within the idiolect.

The term 'paralinguistic' is potentially misleading. It may mislead, first of all, because it may suggest that it refers to something going on at the same time as language; accompanying it but remaining essentially separate. This is not so. The paralinguistic element is just as much part of the total 'message' of an act of speech as the vocabulary or the grammar or the sounds. This is why, for example, novelists find it necessary in writing dialogue to use such 'attributive' verbs as 'snapped', 'drawled', 'hissed' and 'purred'. In interpreting an utterance, in other words, one has to take account not only of *what* was said, but also of *how* it was said. Otherwise, one is liable to mistake joke for insult, or irony for praise. And it is, in any case, impossible in speech to have a *what* without a *how*. The paralinguistic

10 02 95

7 Tx   4.00
          4.00 ST
          0.20 TX
          4.20 TL
          5.00 CA
          0.80 CG

032B0088
     21:24

element, therefore, is not something apart, something added to speech; it is an organic part of it.

The second reason why the term 'paralinguistic' may mislead, is the fact that different writers use it to mean different things. To meet this difficulty we propose to define the term as referring to: transient human activity, vocal or non-vocal, traditionally regarded as lying outside the province of the language scholar, but accompanying language and contributing to the 'message'.

The inclusion of 'transient' as a criterion in this definition may be in need of explanation. It is intended to distinguish such features as tone of voice or gesture, which lead a hearer to conclude that an interlocutor is puzzled or pleased, for example, from those features which enable a hearer to identify permanent attributes of an interlocutor – for instance, that he is American, or is educated – and to exclude the latter from the definition.

Another way of making the same distinction might be to define 'paralinguistic' phenomena as being under the voluntary control of the speaker. However, while this would be true for most paralinguistic behaviour, it is not necessarily true for all. Emotions such as anger, for example, are not always fully under the control of the speaker and consequently may sometimes be associated with involuntary paralinguistic behaviour. For this reason we have preferred the term 'transient'.

The more important vocal paralinguistic devices involve: pitch phenomena, volume, precision, continuity and tempo. We propose to look briefly at each in turn.

Pitch is an essential element of the sound system of English, as it is of every language. Specifically, it is involved in English in the tone, or speech melody, distinctions which are part of intonation. For example, any native speaker will know how to make a given utterance – 'John came late', let us say – either a statement or a question at will, simply by choosing the appropriate speech melody in each case. But in addition to this function within the sound system, pitch also performs important paralinguistic functions: in fact, in two main ways.

We have, first of all, what we might call 'relative pitch height'. Thus the systematic sound melodies we referred to in the last paragraph may be performed by a speaker at normal pitch height; or they may be delivered in either a higher or a lower key. In either of the last two cases, some information additional to the propositional content of the message is indicated. A lower key may suggest an attempt to sound stern, or solemn, among other possibilities. Similarly, a higher key may indicate surprise or excitement.

Two points should be noted in passing. First, the relative height of the pitch melody has to be judged in relation to what is normal for the individual, and individuals differ in this particular. And generally, it is an important principle with regard to paralinguistic behaviour that inter-pretation depends upon reference to what is normal for the individual, rather than to a norm in the language as a whole. This was the main reason, indeed, for discussing the paralinguistic level in relation to style rather than dialect. The second point is that it is impossible to associate raising or lowering of the pitch height, by itself, with a particular meaning. Again, there is a general principle: this time that the various paralinguistic devices act as part of a complex, and not individually. It is impossible, accordingly, to interpret higher or lower relative pitch height without taking account of, for example, facial expression.

The other main way in which pitch functions paralinguistically is with reference to the *extent* of the pitch movement within the speech melody. Consider, for example, the utterance we proposed earlier, 'John came late'. Normally, the syllable selected to carry the speech melody would be 'late', and unmarked statement meaning would call for a relatively shallow fall in pitch on that syllable. It is possible, however, either to exaggerate the extent of the fall, by beginning it higher and ending it lower than normal, or to restrict the fall and make it even more shallow. In either case, something additional to the simple statement is indicated. A lengthened fall could be used to indicate displeasure, for example, and a restricted one, lack of interest.

Characteristically, it appears, exaggerated pitch movement is associated with an increase in volume, whereas restricted movement is quieter. Despite such correspondences, however, volume is in principle a separate paralinguistic device.

Once more, the norm against which deviance, here relative loudness or quietness of voice, is defined is that of the individual. Some people, as we all know, are naturally 'loud-mouthed', while others, among whom perhaps we would like to number ourselves, are 'softly spoken'. But whether we are the one or the other, or somewhere in between, departure from our normal volume is significant. A writer, for example, might report a marked increase in volume by 'thundered' or 'ranted', and a decrease by 'murmured' or 'muttered'; implying in each case some paralinguistic addition to the propositional message. Above all, what loudness indicates is anger: most of us at some time or other have been accused of losing our temper merely because we have increased the volume of our voice. The usual response to the accusation is to deny it; in an unnaturally quiet voice – possibly with clenched teeth. Quietness, in contrast, is associated with intimacy, or perhaps secrecy.

However, the reason for raising or lowering the volume of the voice is not always so simple and obvious. It has been discovered, for example (see Natale, 1975) that there is a strong tendency for interlocutors in a conversation to converge on the same volume, each accommodating to the perceived volume of the other.

Precision is distinct in principle from either pitch or volume. It is a matter, simply put, of the care taken in articulating sounds. Normally when we speak we produce a stream of sound in which certain modifications are never completely made. There is nothing reprehensible in this: it is the nature of normal speech, and causes us little trouble because our perception makes good the losses. It is able to do this because such losses are regular in their occurrence and not haphazard. For example, in normal conversation 'Princes Street' comes out as 'Princestreet', without either speaker or hearer feeling that the articulation has been in any respect faulty.

When speakers wish to increase the clarity of what they are saying, however, perhaps when issuing a warning that must be clearly understood, they may take care to articulate every modification of the stream of sound distinctly. The higher the level of formality, too, the more carefully we feel we have to articulate. A formal job interview, for example, would be more likely to conclude with the interviewee being told 'We shall be writing to you in the next few days . . .', rather than 'We'll be writing . . .'. The response to this is more likely to be 'Thank you' than an informal 'Thanks'.

Less care with articulation than normal produces slurring. It is usually involuntary and indicates tiredness, for instance, or drunkenness.

Continuity depends upon the amount of hesitation and pause. These two should, however, be distinguished from one another. Hesitation, manifested in false starts and new beginnings, occurs most frequently in informal speech, where it is largely involuntary. But it can, with care, be considerably reduced, with a consequent improvement in continuity. A skilful speaker, therefore, can by a voluntary avoidance of hesitation suggest to an interlocutor competence and decisiveness, not only in speech, but also in any matter that happens to be under discussion.

Normally pauses, too, are involuntary, occurring where the speaker is searching for the right word or expression. They may be either silent or filled. Silent pauses tend to be ambiguous in that they may be interpreted by an interlocutor as a signal that the previous speaker has finished speaking, and for this reason pauses are frequently filled. One way to fill them is with a conventional noise, the kind of noise which is usually transcribed as 'er' or 'um'. The other kind of filler is exemplified by 'you see', 'you know', 'I mean' – phrases which occur with varying frequency in informal speech, or with unskilful speakers, to give the speaker breathing space without running the risk of giving up the floor. The better the interlocutors in a situation know one another, the less likely are we to find filled pauses. Silent pauses are, after all, one way of indicating intimacy.

Pauses, like hesitations, can be cut down considerably by a skilful speaker, and avoidance of filled pauses (of both types) may impress a hearer with the speaker's competence. Silent pauses, nevertheless, can be a useful stylistic device which, by keeping a hearer waiting, focuses attention on what follows. It is a feature of the public speaking and interviewee style of a number of leading politicians.

The final vocal paralinguistic device is tempo, or speed of utterance. Each of us has a normal speech tempo, the use of which adds nothing to the propositional content of what we are saying. This tempo is, within fairly narrow limits, under voluntary control, and so may be varied in order to add something to the 'message'. Increase of tempo, for instance, may suggest pressure of time or, perhaps, the pressure of excitement. A slower tempo may suggest boredom. But possibly the most easily observable use of tempo is in sport commentating, where the speaker slows down when nothing decisive is taking place, but gradually increases the tempo when something exciting seems about to happen, thus involving the hearer directly in the tempo of the event.

Non-vocal paralinguistic devices include: facial expression, eye-contact, posture, gesture and physical contact. Once again we shall discuss each briefly in turn.

With all paralinguistic phenomena there is a problem of separating the voluntary from the involuntary, and the signals we give out paralinguistically are often a little of both. Nowhere is this more true than with facial expression, where we often have the feeling that our face is betraying beliefs and attitudes we would prefer to keep hidden: sometimes we just cannot 'keep a straight face'. Nevertheless, we do exercise a large measure of control over what we communicate by means of our faces; and we can communicate a great deal. Broadly speaking, we use our faces to indicate our attitude to what we are saying: that we wish it to be taken seriously, or as a joke; that the sympathy we are offering is sincere; that the story we are telling is to be taken with a pinch of salt. Indeed, so much do people rely upon the facial 'message', that where it contradicts the propositional content of what is being said it is the face that is believed. For example, a severe reprimand delivered with a broad grin would not be taken seriously.

The most compelling feature of the face is the eyes, and eye-contact is an important paralinguistic device. Popularly, the ability to maintain a steady gaze into the eyes of an addressee while speaking is regarded as a sign of candour and integrity. It is for this reason, no doubt, that this ability is cultivated by, among others, second-hand car salesmen and politicians. And it is certainly the reason why people being interviewed on television are advised to look straight at the camera. Anything else can look shifty.

There are many people, however, who, while accepting and even relishing eye-contact with really intimate addressees, such as wives, husbands, sweethearts and children, feel ill at ease maintaining eye-contact while addressing acquaintances. Such people may use eye-contact in a different way; looking away from the addressee most of the time, but coming back from time to time to emphasise a point, and coming back *always* when they reach the end of what they want to say. Silent eye-contact, therefore, can be a signal that the last speaker is ready to 'yield the floor'. The addressee, for their part, keeps their gaze steadily on the speaker all the time, until their turn to speak arrives.

Another device which plays a part in indicating where a speaker's contribution ends is posture, for speakers not merely re-establish eye-contact when they come to the end of what they want to say, but turn their heads, or sometimes their bodies, towards the interlocutor(s), to indicate they are assuming addressee status. Indeed, where there are several interlocutors, this is a way of selecting the next speaker. In addition, there are some situations, certain committee meetings, for example, where a speaker is expected to assume a standing posture when beginning to speak and resume a sitting posture when finished. Change of posture, then, rather than simply a particular posture, may be used to indicate beginnings and ends, and sometimes important points, of a speaker's contribution.

Posture may be used in other ways. One may reinforce an expressed intention to leave by assuming a posture which indicates imminent departure, for example. On the other hand, we all know the visitor who assumes a very comfortable posture in one of our easy chairs late in the evening, indicating by his posture, among other things, that he is in no hurry to leave.

An important part of posture is proximity. Very often *where* we stand is as important as *how*. Most French people, for example, stand closer to addressees than Americans do. As Ms Platt puts it in *The Independent* (18 March 1990, p. 20), 'What they [Americans] don't realise is that the French don't have a bubble of inviolable body-space around them the way we do'. Readers may like to observe their own practice with regard to proximity.

Gesture is really just another kind of posture, the difference being a matter of scale. Posture involves the body as a whole: gesture only parts of the body, particularly the hands and arms. We may, for example, emphasise a point by a strong gesture with an arm; indicate indifference with a shrug of the shoulder; or reinforce an agreement with a nod. English speakers are generally more sparing with gesture than are, for example, speakers of Italian, and in England at least too ostentatious a use of gesture in conversation would be considered inappropriate. Nevertheless, politicians throughout the world exploit the impact of specific, choreographed gestures, which have become part of the language of persuasion.

Finally, we come to physical contact, or touch, as a paralinguistic device. Here the English tend to be reticent, though other speakers of English appear to be much less inhibited. Perhaps the most obvious example of paralinguistic touch is shaking hands; something the English do much less than most Europeans. But even for the English shaking hands appears to be a necessary accompaniment in certain speech situations: on being introduced, when congratulating someone, or greeting guests at a reception. Other kinds of paralinguistic touch include: clapping a friend on the back, tugging at a sleeve to attract attention, putting one's arms round a friend's shoulders in a gesture of comfort. *Who* can be touched, *where* and *when*, and what it all means, is a complex subject. Once again we invite readers to observe their own practice, as well as that of others.

Stylistic modification of the sound system, i.e. the accent, has been a popular area of research (see particularly Labov, Trudgill, Giles), and looks like becoming even more popular in the future. Much research so far may be interpreted as demonstrating, broadly, that each of us (as a member of some socio-regional grouping) has a 'normal' accent; that 'normal' implies, at least for certain crucial features, a range of possible realisations, rather than a unique realisation; and, further, that variation in the realisation of these features is motivated by differences in non-linguistic context. Future research will explore these hypotheses and attempt to identify, on the one hand, the variant features and, on the other, the causative contextual factors.

One of the most frequently quoted examples of accent mobility concerns the pronunciation of certain 'marker' features in New York (Labov, 1966). One feature studied, for example, was the 'th' at the beginning of such words as 'thing', 'three', 'thrush', for which three possible realisations were recognised: (1) the pronunciation most native speakers would regard as 'correct', that of the Greek letter θ; (2) a stop pronunciation, i.e. 't'; and (3) a pronunciation in which the stop was followed by audible friction; also often heard, for example, in 'broad' Liverpool speech. The pronunciation habits of four class groups (lower, working, lower middle and upper middle) were studied with respect to this feature, at four levels of formality. It was found, first, that all groups varied their pronunciation regularly so as to give a higher proportion of 'correct' realisations as the formality increased and, secondly, that each class group had a unique range of possible realisations. The ranges did overlap, so that the lower-class realisation in a formal situation corresponded to middle-class realisations at a less formal level, for example, but the overall range for any given group was quite distinct.

Another potential source of accent mobility has been suggested by Giles (1973), who argues that there is a measurable tendency for speakers to modify their pronunciation in the direction of that of their addressee, so that the accents of interlocutors converge. However, convergence of this kind is not a simple matter, since it must take account of a number of complicating factors, such as linguistic prestige, social status, accent loyalty and, perhaps most of all, the sensitivity and flexibility of the speaker.

Vocabulary modification is probably the most obvious and accessible aspect of stylistic variety, and so vocabulary commonly figures prominently in discussions of styles. Unfortunately, these treatments of vocabulary are seldom as illuminating as they might be, because of a tendency to confound the referential element in word choice with the contextual. For example, it might convincingly be argued that words like 'crankshaft', 'ignition' and 'transmission' all belong to a particular register, let us call it 'the register of automotive engineering', implying that the choice of these words is contextually motivated. But that is clearly not so. When the word 'crankshaft' is used, for instance, it is entirely because that is what the thing referred to is properly and uniquely called; in other words, the choice is referentially determined.

This confusion is, in fact, a prime source of the vagueness to be found in discussions of register. It arises for the very simple reason that the theory of language with which the notion of register originates (see Halliday, McIntosh and Strevens, 1964) emphasises the contextual dimension of language use, but makes no provision whatsoever for the referential. As a consequence, there is no basis for distinguishing the contextual from the referential, and hence no real basis in the theory of register for dealing convincingly even with the contextual aspect of vocabulary choice.

From our point of view, however, the matter is relatively simple: stylistic modification of the vocabulary is concerned with choice among items for purely contextual reasons. In other words, either the choice is made from a set of items which all share the same reference, or, alternatively, where the reference has no real significance. In either case reference is not a factor in the choice.

The term 'item' should be noted in the above definition. It is intended to allow for the inclusion of phrases and expressions of various kinds, as well as single words. In an informal conversation, for example, one might hear expressions such as the following: 'start from scratch', 'that sort of thing', 'something like that', 'you're joking', 'on the quiet', 'hang on', 'fed up', 'so he says'. Any recorded conversation will reveal many more.

Many of these examples of conversational expressions, incidentally, also exemplify non-significant reference. They would occur almost entirely for their appropriateness to a conversational context. As an illustration of the other kind of choice, from a set of items all having the same reference but differing in their contextual appropriateness, consider the many alternatives to the term 'jail', such as 'calaboose', 'clink', 'cooler', 'glasshouse', 'nick', 'penitentiary' and 'stir'. Similar lists of alternatives could be given for Englishman ('Brit', 'John Bull', 'Pommy', 'Sassenach' and 'Tommy'), marriage ('match', 'matrimony', 'union' and 'wedlock') and wife ('better half', 'good lady', 'helpmate' and 'spouse').

It would not be difficult to multiply examples of stylistically motivated vocabulary variety; for example, in greetings, in the use of taboo words, or technical terms, or slang. But perhaps the most immediately familiar illustration concerns the way in which people address one another, and refer to one another, according to differing status, formality or relationships. Let us take as an actual example a university department consisting of one professor, one elderly senior lecturer, four lecturers and one secretary. In informal situations, the professor and all the lecturers address one another and refer to one another by the first name (FN), the secretary is addressed and referred to by FN, but addresses the professor and the senior lecturer, and refers to them, by title + last name (TLN), while the other lecturers she addresses and refers to by FN. All the students refer to the professor, and address him, either as (the) professor or by TLN; almost all address the senior lecturer by TLN, but a few use FN, and rather more refer to him by FN + LN; many, especially among the postgraduate students, address the other lecturers by FN and almost all refer to them by FN + LN. In more formal situations, however, things change. The professor and lecturers address one another, and refer to one another by TLN. The students address and refer to all the staff, including the secretary, by TLN. Likewise, things change according to who is present: for example, a student who normally refers to the senior lecturer by FN + LN, would use TLN in his presence.

It would not be very helpful to attempt to link the complex variable network of relationships and status to the complicated choices of address or reference terms at the gross level of situation, i.e. 'register'. Clearly, what we really have is a collection of individuals, each operating his or her own (potentially) unique address and reference system, which he or she can modify at will in order to communicate an attitude of, for example, respect, affection, dislike, or distance. And the others understand the various messages because, though they each operate a slightly different system, they all recognise identical principles. It should be borne in mind, too, that the address system operates in conjunction with paralinguistic and linguistic clues, so that one is seldom in doubt about whether a given term on a given occasion means one thing or another.

There is certainly an element of predictability: secretaries usually address professors by TLN, for example. But the individual is always in control. It is not unknown for some secretaries to call their professors something else, either all the time or just part of the time! We do better, therefore, to see choice of address or reference term as within the individual systems rather than as imposed by an external situation.

In dealing with dialect we asserted that it was very unusual to find anyone who, having mastered Standard English, remained in full control of a consistent regional or class dialect. But what does happen is that speakers retain control of enough dialect features to give the impression, to themselves as well as others, that they are familiar with the dialect. Mainly it is a matter of accent: most speakers are able to vary along a continuum between (broad) dialect pronunciation and some kind of more general system. But vocabulary also has a dialect dimension. For example, with regard to address again, women in south-east Scotland are not surprised to hear themselves addressed as 'hen', whereas in Sheffield it is more likely to be 'my duck'. And generally speaking dialect terms are an option for many speakers.

Nor is it only a matter of address terms. For example, it would not be considered out of place for a Scot who normally spoke Standard English to observe that a speech was 'gey driech' (rather dry), or to refer to turnips as 'tumshies', a stream as a 'burn', or a child as a 'bairn', if the occasion called for a dialect style. The 'message', normally, in these cases is one of solidarity: 'I am one of you'.

The final element in the style complex is grammar. In the past, the textbooks commonly used in schools implied that correctness in language use is a simple matter of conformity to a set of more or less well-defined rules of grammar, which it is the duty of the English teacher to impart and impose. More recently, transformational-generative grammar, though its interpretation of 'rules' is considerably more sophisticated, clearly identifies the immediate task of linguistics as the provision of a complex set of rules which will define or enumerate (i.e. generate) all and only the grammatical sentences of the language, without any reference whatsoever to contextual or situational considerations. Whatever the merits of these approaches, and whatever the arguments offered in their support – the need to teach error-free English in the first case; the possibility ultimately of describing certain species-specific properties of the human mind, in the second – it is evident that they both ignore an important factor: the extent to which the 'correctness' of a given utterance is a matter of its stylistic appropriateness to the situation in which it is used. Where a conflict arises between what the textbooks would regard as grammatical and what is appropriate, it is the latter, always, that ought to be respected.

Such an assertion should not be read as counselling grammatical anarchy. There are structural regularities to be observed in English, as in every human language. However, description of those regularities does not by itself define their correctness.

Consider, for example, how we might get someone to give us a newspaper we want. We might do it by using an interrogative sentence: 'Have you finished with that paper?', 'Would you mind passing the paper?', 'Is that this morning's paper?', 'Has anyone seen my paper?'; or by an imperative: 'Give me the paper (please)', 'Pass that paper over here'; or by a declarative: 'I'd like the paper'; 'I'm looking for the paper'; 'You know I always have the paper at breakfast-time'. The 'correctness' of any one of these possibilities is really relative, dependent upon the circumstances in which it is used. Since grammars have no way of taking circumstances into account, however, they are obliged to define sentences such as these as absolutely 'correct', entirely by reference to their structural possibilities.

But that is not all. The sentences quoted above are all grammatically 'complete', and so represent the unit (i.e. the sentence) grammars have traditionally undertaken to account for. There are many situations, however, where an 'incomplete' sentence would be more likely, and more effective: 'Got the paper?', 'Finished with the paper?', 'My paper, please', or, simply 'Paper!'. There is no doubt that utterances of this kind may be situationally 'correct'. Moreover, they are strictly speaking grammatical too – unlike, for example, 'The paper got?' or 'Finish with paper?'. But grammar books and grammar theories have usually found it impossible to account for them. Not only does a strictly structural definition of correctness fail to recognise the importance of the circumstances of particular situations, therefore, but it fails to include a great deal of normal English, even in its own terms.

In any given situation, then, we always have to decide just what is called for and be able to respond accordingly. We have to distinguish those situations which demand complete sentences ('Would you prefer tea or coffee?') from those in which phrases, parts of phrases, or single words are appropriate ('Tea or coffee?'); those situations where simple sentences would be more effective ('Mary's tired. We'd better go') than complex ('My little girl seems to be getting tired, and so, if you wouldn't mind, I think we'd better go home'). We have to be able to judge, according to circumstances, whether to use an adjective clause ('who was sitting in the corner'), or a prepositional phrase ('in the corner'); an adverbial clause ('when he had finished') or a phrase ('a moment later'); whether or not to include various kinds of sentence link (anaphora, lexical repetition, adverbial connectives such as 'however', 'on the other hand', 'as we have already seen'); whether or not to use an adjective ('my (dear) wife') or an adjective clause ('the woman *to whom I have been happily married for x years*'). The possibilities are very numerous and evidently choosing among them demands a reliable knowledge of the structure of the language, but such knowledge is not to be confused with the contents of any grammar book. More important, mere structural knowledge is not enough.

So far in our discussion of style we have been concerned with language, and with the kind of variation that occurs there; at the paralinguistic level and in the sound system, the vocabulary and the grammar. We turn now to the non-language aspect of style, to the situation, in fact, in order to try to identify there the factors to which the language variation responds.

We may begin by noting that any speech situation involves of necessity:

(1) Participants, i.e. speaker and addressee(s). Speaking to oneself is, of course, an exceptional case, where the same person is both speaker and addressee at the same time. It must be remembered, too, that in many speech situations it is normal for the participants to act alternately as speaker or addressee.
(2) A topic of discourse.
(3) A setting, i.e. an occasion and a place.
(4) Other language activity. At any given moment in a speech situation, stylistic choice will be determined to some extent by what has been said previously, by whom, and in what style.

Each of these elements of situation is a variable, and they all, to a greater or lesser degree, influence the stylistic choices we make whenever we speak. These are the factors we seek to clarify.

We should not wish to give the impression that individual factors act independently. If the relationship between situation and style were as simple as that, then clearly there would be little difficulty about identifying particular features of style with unique elements of situation; or for that matter a whole 'register' with a total situation. But things are not so simple. What happens is that a language item (associated with a particular gesture or facial expression, embedded in a particular grammatical structure, uttered in this or that accent) is a response to a whole complex of situational factors: these participants, that topic, this setting. Change *any* situational factor and the entire style complex may have to be rearranged: a different item, with or without change of gesture, structure and accent. Despite the danger of oversimplification, however, we propose to consider each element separately.

In discussing the way in which the participants in a language situation may influence the language used, we have to start from the relationship between speaker and addressee.

Relationships in fact vary along a continuum, from close to remote. At one end are our husbands, wives, children, parents and other intimates, and at the other end a queen or a president, perhaps, with acquaintances and senior and junior colleagues spaced out appropriately along the way. The corresponding stylistic continuum ranges from intimate to explicit: the more remote the relationship, the greater the necessity for explicitness at every level.

Intimate language is characteristically inexplicit; so that utterances need not be complete sentences and structure will tend to be simple, vague words such as 'nice' and 'thing' may be used, and pronunciation will tend to be relaxed: 'dusman' rather than 'dustman', and 'tempence' instead of 'ten pence', for example. But inexplicitness is not the only characteristic of this style. Slang, colloquialisms, cryptic allusions of various kinds, false starts, slips of the tongue and silent pauses are also very probable. Movement in the direction of remoteness in the speaker–addressee relationship will entail progressive removal of all these features, together with an increase of complexity in structure, of accuracy in vocabulary and precision in pronunciation.

One important element in the relationship between speaker and addressee is the amount of shared knowledge, and it would be easy to make the mistake of supposing it the only important element: the closer the relationship the greater the shared knowledge and, hence, the less need to be explicit. Other considerations must, however, be taken into account here. The technical knowledge shared by colleagues at work, for example, is likely to be much more extensive than that shared by husband and wife, though the latter relationship would normally be the closer. Husband and wife, on the other hand, may be expected to share more knowledge of matters directly relating to the family. Shared knowledge, and its influence on choice of language, is not a mere matter of closeness or remoteness of relationship, therefore, since it also thus involves the topic of discourse. And, by the same token, the effect of the speaker–addressee relationship is not to be attributed solely to the shared knowledge of the participants. Other factors, affection for example, play an important part.

In addition to the general influence of the relationship of the participants to one another, there are particular influences associated with speaker and addressee separately. In the case of the speaker there appear to be two factors to consider: role and purpose.

The term 'role' is meant to suggest that in our everyday lives each of us must play a variety of parts. At one time a person may be acting as a teacher, at another time as a committee chairman, at yet another as a patient, for example. It is impossible to know how many such roles society recognises but we all have to learn a large number of them, our personal repertoire, and every time we speak we assume whichever of them is appropriate to the situation. Among other things, and perhaps above all, this means choosing appropriate language.

Choices may have to be made at every level. Consider, for example, the role of interviewee at the job interview. Good interviewees will wish to give the right impression of alertness, intelligence and respect for the interviewers, and will do this most effectively by paying careful attention to posture, facial expression, articulation, tempo, and indeed to all paralinguistic signals. They will also probably modify their pronunciation in the direction of the local prestige accent if this is not already their normal accent; so that in England they will tend to modify in the direction of RP. Their vocabulary, too, will be chosen with care, so that they might prefer 'recalcitrant', 'ill advised' and 'impertinent' to 'awkward', 'hare-brained' and 'cheeky'. Likewise our hypothetical interviewees would probably select grammatical structures with a due regard for their effect: 'I am aware that the view you express is widely held, but I personally favour the alternative view proposed by Felstein, that . . .' rather than 'You are mistaken', though the latter might be entirely appropriate in a different context, such as a discussion among friends.

The term 'purpose' is transparent. It simply refers to what speakers in a given situation intend their words to do: persuade, perhaps, or threaten, or instruct, or seduce. Achieving a purpose calls for appropriate language. An obvious example is provided by television commercials, where the purpose is to persuade the viewer to buy particular products. Among other things this may call for careful attention to accent: a Welsh accent to sell beer in Wales, a Yorkshire one to sell it in Yorkshire, but an RP accent for Martini. Vocabulary, too, is very important. The popular words change, but fashions have included 'silk', 'turbo', 'ozone friendly', 'green', 'natural' and 'additive free'. The label on the Marmite jar used to have the words 'Full of natural goodness – no additives'. It now has 'Contains B Vitamins – 100% Vegetarian'. At the grammatical end we find simple structures and lots of repetition. The study of television commercials in order to discover what language choices advertisers make, and why, is in fact very instructive. This matter will be taken up again in Chapter 6.

Though we shall not have enough space to discuss 'purpose' as extensively as it merits, and shall have to leave it to the reader to find further examples from their own observation and experience, there is one particular purpose about which we must say at least a few words. This is the purpose which is usually called 'phatic communion'.

Briefly, a surprising proportion of everyday language behaviour has no other purpose than to signal to an addressee the speaker's willingness to co-operate socially. This signal is what is meant by 'phatic communion'. Characteristically, it occurs between friends and acquaintances to maintain their relationship. We meet a friend, for example, and say 'Good morning', and we chat for a few moments, perhaps about the weather or work or the health of members of the family. We may then go on to engage in serious discussion, or we may simply take our leave with some well-worn ritual phrase: 'Cheers', 'So long', 'Goodbye', etc. The serious discussion is not phatic communion, but all the rest is. None of it is really more than reassuring noise, used solely to reinforce the friendly relationship.

But maintaining existing relationships is not the only possible function of phatic communion. It may occur between strangers, for example, either for mutual reassurance or as a means of developing and establishing a relationship: all our friends were strangers once, and but for phatic communion would probably have remained so. Nor is friendliness a necessary factor, either as a condition or a consequence, for people who dislike one another may yet engage in a certain amount of phatic communion, if only to keep hostility from developing into aggression.

The language used may seem to lack intellectual content, but phatic communion should not for that reason be dismissed as of little consequence. Maintaining friendly or supportive relations with others is very important for all of us, and someone who is unable to engage in phatic communion is likely to have few friends. The apparently meaningless expressions we so often use in our encounters with others, therefore, are not meaningless at all but highly meaningful; and an essential element in 'knowing the language'.

For the second participant in a language situation we have used the term 'addressee', which is a convenient term but rather misleading, in that there may be more than one. Moreover, the number of addressees can be stylistically critical. The kind of informal language we earlier described as appropriate to close relationships, for example, is really only possible among relatively small groups, which is why successful dinner parties, and tutorials for that matter, call for careful limitation of numbers. Larger groups, even of close friends, trigger off changes in style. We may use greater volume, exaggerated gestures, posture and tone of voice, and modified vocabulary and grammar.

An even more important stylistic consideration than numbers, however, is what we shall call 'relative status'; just how we stand in relation to the person we are speaking to.

Relative status is mainly a question of whether the addressee is perceived by the speaker to be inferior, superior or equal on some social scale. Other considerations may certainly have to be taken into account, in particular, whether the speaker and addressee are male or female, young or old. Such considerations will affect paralinguistic behaviour such as posture, gesture, tone of voice and volume, but are likely also to influence vocabulary choice. There are, for example, many expressions which men will use fairly freely among themselves but avoid in the presence of women, though taboos are not as powerful as once they were. Likewise, many modern colloquial and slang expressions might be avoided with old people, to whom they could be obscure or meaningless. Nevertheless, the main factor in relative status does seem to be whether, and to what extent, speakers perceive themselves to be superior, or inferior to the addressee(s). When we hear someone say irately 'Who do you think you are talking to?' it is usually this which is in question, not age or sex.

Relative status may influence stylistic choice at every level. Where you stand, how you stand, and even whether you stand, for example, will all reflect your perception of the status of your addressee relative to yourself, as will such other paralinguistic choices as your articulation, tone of voice, pitch and facial expression. Your sound system, too, is likely to reflect the same perception: almost everyone has a 'posher' accent for addressing superiors, for example. Vocabulary will also be affected: address terms, reference terms for yourself and others (first name, nickname, title and last name), and whether or not you use colloquialisms and slang.

Nor is it difficult to exemplify differences of structure according to the perceived relative status of addressees. Consider, for example, some of the different ways we might phrase a request to have a door shut when for some reason we are unable to do it ourselves.

(1) Door!
(2) Shut the door (will you) (please)?
(3) I could do without the draught from that door.
(4) May we have the door shut (please)?
(5) Would you mind closing the door (please)?
(6) I wonder if you would mind closing the door.
(7) I'm sorry to trouble you, but could I ask you to close the door for me, please.

Many other possibilities remain, of course, but looking just at the examples listed, given in ascending order according to status of addressee, we see that the differences involve mood (statement, question, exclamation and imperative), length and complexity. Note, too, the difference in style between the inclusion or non-inclusion of 'please'.

The influence of the topic of discourse, which is the situational factor we must discuss next, is most frequently quoted with reference to vocabulary choice; which is why discussions of 'register' are frequently supported by assertions that, for example, the terms 'foul', 'striker' and 'goal' are part of the 'register of football'. We argued earlier, however, that choice of a particular vocabulary item because that is what the thing you want to talk about is called has no stylistic implications. Undoubtedly, when you are discussing football, or the weather, or nuclear physics, or any other specialist topic, you do have to use the appropriate terms if you are to identify clearly and unambiguously the concepts and things you are talking about. But this is a matter of reference, not style. Style is involved only where choice is made between one term and another *when both, in the context, refer to the same thing*.

The influence on style of the topic of discourse may be considerably less important than is commonly believed. As we saw earlier, it may be a factor in deciding how much common knowledge is shared, and consequently what may be left unsaid or inexplicit; affecting particularly in this way vocabulary and grammar. Beyond that, there may be particular topics which call for a certain degree of delicacy in selection of vocabulary such as death and sex. But here, too, the identity of the addressee must be taken into account. Most of us have experienced at some time the difficulty of finding the right words in which to express our condolences for a recent bereavement. Sensitive speakers (or writers) will take account not only of the fact of death, but also of their relationship to the addressee, and to the deceased, as well as the age and sex of the addressee, and even his or her religious affiliation. By itself, therefore, the topic of discourse seems to be of limited stylistic significance.

Probably its main influence would be claimed for the choice between technical and non-technical language. With many topics, speakers have a choice of terms. They may, for example, talk about 'a contractile, wave-like movement of the muscles of the oesophagus', or about 'swallowing'; about 'watery secretions of the salivary gland', or 'spit'. Sciences such as botany, zoology and geology offer many alternatives of this kind. Even so, the identity of the addressee will usually be the deciding factor, not the topic. The botanist lecturing to a class of students is likely to stick closely to the scientific names for the plants being discussed – they are not merely names, of course, but also classificatory terms – but in talking about the same plants with country people the popular names will be used.

The next factor, setting, is, stylistically speaking, much more important.

The primary consideration is: what is the *occasion*? Are the participants in the speech situation attending a wedding reception or a funeral? taking part in a conversation, or in Question Time in the House? engaged in a trial or a consultation? On certain occasions particular roles have their language narrowly prescribed, leaving little and sometimes no choice to the speaker. Most English speakers would probably be able to identify the occasions for the following, for example:

(1)   I name this ship *Morning Star*. May God bless her and all who sail in her.

(2)   I now pronounce you man and wife.

(3)   Is the Honourable Member aware . . .?
(4)   Move to the left in threes. Left turn.
(5)   I see a tall, dark stranger entering your life.

Prescription may extend right through to the paralinguistic signals. The drill sergeant of (4), for example, is expected to adopt a particular posture, increase the volume of his voice, extend his pitch on the penultimate syllable and apply extra strong stress to his final syllable.

Other occasions are less prescriptive, offering the speaker much greater freedom of choice. Nevertheless, the freedom is probably only relative. The male speaker at a wedding reception, for instance, must not sound like a lecturer with a class of students. He must stand, usually with a glass in his hand, and must adopt an appropriate facial expression – communicating happiness and goodwill – select the right tone of voice, varying it according to the content of his speech between jocular and sentimental, refer to bride and groom by their familiar family names ('Pete and Liz' rather than 'Peter and Elizabeth', for example), include the assembled guests in certain of his sentiments by means of the 'inclusive we', and avoid complexity of thought or utterance. The lecturer must also stand, but is free to walk up and down, lean confidentially over a desk or remain bolt upright if he wishes. He may permit himself a smile occasionally, when he feels he has been particularly witty, but will avoid beaming on his students like someone's inebriated uncle. He will take care to speak clearly, vary his tempo and tone and attempt to use his silent pauses, perhaps, to indicate particularly noteworthy points. Reference to others will normally be by second name only, even where the reference is to a close friend, and complex thoughts will be married carefully to appropriate structure so that connections are made explicit by the use of such link-words as 'because', 'unless', 'whenever' and 'accordingly'.

Many occasions are associated with a characteristic *place*: lessons with a classroom, trials with a courtroom. In such cases 'place' cannot be considered a distinct factor in the setting. Conversations, however, are entirely free with regard to place, and may occur virtually anywhere, and where they occur may influence the language used. Speakers who are on home ground, for example, may feel called upon to indicate to the addressee by posture, tone and other paralinguistic signals that the latter is welcome. They may even give what appear to be orders: 'Find yourself a comfortable chair', 'Help yourself to the Scotch'. The visitor, in turn, must know how to play the role of polite guest: 'Goodness, that's far too much'. Conversation following a chance meeting in the street will probably be confined to commonplace remarks about the weather or some topic of mutual interest. A conversation between the same people in the club or pub, on the other hand, will probably permit lengthy and complex exchanges and even tolerate long, silent pauses between contributions.

The final situational factor we have to consider is what we have referred to as 'other language activity'. The point we wish to make is that language is not something distinct from the situation in which it occurs but an organic part of that situation, not merely because of its propositional content, but also because of its style. Often, indeed, it is the style which identifies a situation as quarrel or discussion, consultation or conversation, instruction or reprimand. Participants in a speech situation, therefore, need to be sensitive to stylistic signals at every level, and be prepared to respond appropriately. This is not to say that one speaker is a prisoner of the language activity of another person or persons and must respond in kind. He may, for example, detecting quarrel signals, seek stylistically to mollify his addressee(s). Alternatively, he can if he chooses escalate the quarrel, by adopting a more aggressive stance, 'raising' his voice and using pejorative terms of various kinds, for example. In other words, speakers who are conscious of a variety of stylistic options, and skilful in their selection, are able to exercise more control over the situation than the situation does over them.

Dialogue, therefore, is interactive in nature, the participants continuously assessing the situation and adjusting their stylistic choices to accord with their assessment. Sometimes participants make the wrong choices, perhaps because they misjudge the situation. An addressee may imagine a slight in something that has been said, for example, and react accordingly; or a speaker misjudges the relative status of the other participant(s) with the result that what was intended to be generous and sincere instead sounds patronising. Alternatively, a speaker may blunder through lack of the necessary stylistic resources to respond appropriately to a particular situation. Many people, for example, find it difficult to know what to say when faced with an addressee of an unfamiliar type; perhaps someone of a different race or class.

We respond as skilfully as our resources allow, then, to the situation *as it appears to us*, often on the evidence of what has been said and how it has been said. Sometimes the objective 'facts' of the situation correspond closely to our perception of them, and then it is tempting to see the 'facts' themselves as imposing the stylistic choices. A court of law, for example, permits little choice as to how the judge will be addressed or questions responded to; and, to take a less exotic example, we seem to have few alternatives in responding to an introduction. However, in the last analysis, the speaker is always in charge. There is ultimately no way, for example, of preventing a witness from making an indignant outburst if he feels he is being wrongly accused of lying, though the judge will always attempt to rebuke or persuade him into seeing things differently.

We must repeat what we said earlier in this chapter: the operation of the situational variables we have discussed, their interrelationships with one another, and their influence on stylistic choice are extremely complex; so complex that nobody has as yet produced a convincing theory which would provide a coherent and illuminating explanation of it all. Linguists have usually reacted to the complexity by devising some theoretical mechanism to justify its exclusion. In this way they have been able to construct systematic and coherent theories, which, however, are able to tell us virtually nothing about how language functions in everyday, real-life communication. Even those linguists who have stressed the importance of situation, such as the followers of the English linguist J. R. Firth, seem to have made little headway in dealing with the multidimensional continua involved, although they have drawn attention to the phenomena that any really comprehensive theory of language would have to account for.

Nor do we claim to have done more in the present chapter. We have attempted to establish that language is subject to virtually continuous variation along several dimensions, in response to variable situational factors, which include the language activity itself as part of an organic whole. We have not sought to provide answers but rather to suggest questions. We believe that these questions will prove fascinating to anyone interested in investigating how language really works.

Additional Reading

Abercrombie, D. (1967), *Elements of General Phonetics* (Edinburgh: Edinburgh University Press).

Argyle, M. (1967), *The Psychology of Interpersonal Behaviour* (Harmondsworth: Penguin).

Austin, J. L. (1962), *How to Do Things with Words* (Oxford: O.U.P.).

Birdwhistell, R. L. (1952), *An Introduction to Kinesics: An Annotation System of Body Motion and Gesture* (Louisville, Ky.: University of Louisville Press).

Birdwhistell, R. L. (1973), *Kinesics and Context* (Harmondsworth: Penguin).

Brook, G. L. (1973), *Varieties of English* (London: Macmillan).

Brown, J. C. (1963), *Techniques of Persuasion* (Harmondsworth: Penguin).

Brown, P. and Levinson, S. C. (1987), *Politeness* (Cambridge: C.U.P.).

Brown, R. and Gilman, A. (1960), 'The pronouns of power and solidarity', in T. A. Sebeok (ed.) (1960), *Style in Language* (New York & London: Wiley), pp. 253–76.

Brown, R. and Ford, M. (1961), 'Address in American English', *Journal of Abnormal and Social Psychology*, vol. 62, pp. 375–85.

Cicourel, A. V. (1973), *Cognitive Sociology: Language Meaning in Social Interaction* (Harmondsworth: Penguin).

Coulthard, M. (1977), *An Introduction to Discourse Analysis* (London: Longman).

Crystal, D. and Davy, D. (1969), *Investigating English Style* (London: Longman).

Ervin-Tripp, S. (1976), 'Is Sybil there? The structure of some American directives', *Language in Society*, vol. 5, pp. 25–65.

Ferguson, C. (1976), 'The structure and use of politeness formulas', *Language in Society*, vol. 5, pp. 137–51.

Giglioli, P. P. (ed.) (1972), *Language and Social Context* (Harmondsworth: Penguin).

Giles, H. (1973), 'Accent mobility: a model and some data', *Anthropological Linguistics*, vol. 15, no. 2, pp. 87–105.

Giles, H. and Powesland, P. F. (1975), *Speech Style and Social Evaluation* (London: Academic Press).

Goffman, E. (1972), *Interaction Ritual* (Harmondsworth: Penguin).

Goffman, E. (1981), *Forms of Talk* (Oxford: Blackwell).

Gregory, M. and Carroll, S. (1978), *Language and Situation* (London: Routledge and Kegan Paul).

Gumperz, J. J. (1982), *Discourse Strategies* (Cambridge: C.U.P.).

Halliday, M. A. K. (1973), *Explorations in the Function of Language* (London: Edward Arnold).

Halliday, M. A. K. (1975), *Learning how to Mean: Explorations in the Development of Language* (London: Edward Arnold).

Halliday, M. A. K. et al. (1964), *The Linguistic Sciences and Language Teaching* (London: Longmans).

Halliday, M. A. K. and Hasan, R. (1976), *Cohesion in English* (London: Longmans).

Halliday, M. A. K. and Hasan, R. (1989), *Language, Context and Text: Aspects of Language in a Social-semiotic Perspective* (Oxford: O.U.P.).

Joos, M. (1961), *The Five Clocks* (New York: Harcourt).

Labov, W. (1966), *The Social Stratification of English in New York City* (Washington, D.C.: Center for Applied Linguistics).

Lakoff, R. (1975), *Language and Woman's Place* (New York and London: Harper Row).

Laver, J. and Hutcheson, S. (eds) (1972), *Communication in Face to Face Interaction* (Harmondsworth: Penguin).

Lyons, J. (1966), 'Firth's theory of meaning', in C. E. Bazell et al. (eds), *In Memory of J. R. Firth* (London: Longmans), pp. 288–302.

Mitchell, T. F. (1975), *Principles of Firthian Linguistics* (London: Longmans).

Natale, M. (1975), 'Convergence of mean vocal intensity in dyadic communication as a function of social desirability', *Journal of Personality and Social Psychology*, vol. 32, no. 5, pp. 790–804.

Robinson, W. P. (1972), *Language and Social Behaviour* (Harmondsworth: Penguin).

Spender, D. (1980), *Man Made Language* (London: Routledge and Kegan Paul).

Trudgill, P. (1974), *The Social Differentiation of English in Norwich* (Cambridge: C.U.P.).

Wardhaugh, R. (1983), *How Conversation Works* (Oxford: Blackwell).
Widdowson, H. G. (1983), *Learning Purpose and Language Use* (Oxford: O.U.P.).

5 English and the Media

Much of our regular language activity takes place in direct, person-to-person situations; in dialogues of one kind or another, or in correspondence. In addition, most of these personal encounters are interactive, two-way affairs in which we alternate between the roles of producer and receiver. But not all our language activity is of this kind. Some of it, and an increasing amount in complex, modern societies, is of a more impersonal kind, which involves most of us only as receivers, never producers, and which addresses us not as individual persons but as members of an undifferentiated mass, the audience for what are popularly called 'the media'. In this chapter we propose to look at the kind of language variation to be found in the various media and to discuss the effect media language has on the language as a whole.

By the 'media' we mean, of course, newspapers, radio, television and films. We shall discuss them separately, though we are aware that each influences the others and that, for example, words like 'aggro', 'bionic', 'consumer' and 'giro' appear first in one, spread to the others and eventually become part of the vocabulary of nearly every one of us. And we shall discuss them in the order in which we have listed them.

First then, the newspapers. Perhaps we should draw attention to the speed with which the industry can change. Limiting our comments to the decade between 1980 and 1990, we can mention six changes. In 1980, Fleet Street, where virtually all English dailies were printed, was used as a synonym for the Press. On 9 April, 1989, the last newspaper, the *Sunday Express*, was published there. In the early 1980s, most dailies were set by hand using technologies which had changed little in 100 years. Since the publication of Eddie Shah's *Today* on 4 March, 1986, all major newspapers have introduced computer-aided technology. Children's papers such as *Early Times* have begun to be published. On 24 February, 1987, Robert Maxwell, owner of the *Mirror* started the first 24-hour daily, the London *Daily News*. (It failed.) In November 1988, a new left-wing paper, *The Post*, was offered to the public. After thirty-three issues, it was closed down. And finally, the decade has seen the introduction of a new quality daily, the *Independent*, two new quality Sundays, the *Correspondent* and the *Independent on Sunday*, and a weekend paper, the *European*.

Recent figures suggest that people in Britain buy approximately 15.5 million daily papers. In content, presentation and readership, these fall into two main groups. At what is often called the 'quality' end of the market are *The Times*, the *Guardian*, the *Telegraph*, the *Independent* and *The Financial Times*, which together have a circulation of just over 3 million. At the 'popular' end come the *Daily Express*, the *Daily Mail, Today*, the *Mirror*, the *Sun* and the *Star*, with the *Mirror* and the *Sun* accounting for over 45 per cent of all daily papers sold in Britain.

In addition to the 'nationals', that is, papers which are circulated with only minor differences throughout the country, Britain has a number of local dailies. Yorkshire, for example, has the *Yorkshire Post* and Edinburgh has its *Scotsman*, both of them enjoying a high reputation for quality. Northern Ireland also has local dailies, but in keeping with the traditions of the province, one, *The Newsletter*, addresses itself almost exclusively to Protestants, while another, *The Irish News*, is read mainly by Catholics. Across the Atlantic, the American tradition of freedom and independence in journalism has produced a large number of local dailies, but until Rupert Murdoch introduced *Today*, the United States had no 'national' newspaper that was designed to incorporate regional variations and thus appeal to the widest possible American readership. Mention of Rupert Murdoch, an Australian press baron who owns the *Sun, Today* and *The Times* in Britain, should remind us of two points. The first is that much of the 'news' that all English speakers read is controlled by a small number of media magnates, thus ensuring that anglophones tend to read about the same world events. And secondly, newspapers and their controllers not only determine what we know about the world in terms of politics, economics and natural disasters, but they also help to shape the way we speak and even the way we think about them.

An examination of just *what* a given newspaper chooses to tell its readers can be very revealing. On 11 January, 1990, for example, we compared the 44-page broadsheet *Guardian* (then costing 35 pence) with the 52-page tabloid *Sun* (costing 25 pence). There was considerable overlap in the subjects covered. Both papers had sections devoted to finance, employment opportunities, sport, correspondence, radio and television, weather and women, but the similarities were more apparent than real. The *Guardian* supplied 'Financial News' whereas the *Sun* had '£ Sun Money'; the 'Guardian Women' section narrated one story only, the success of the all-women team in the Whitbread Round the World Yacht Race. The *Sun*, on the other hand, used five pages to highlight an Englishwoman in Romania, sex and medical problems, dieting practices of the stars, as well as a photograph of a half-naked young man thought to have 'the perfect back'. In this book, however, we are less concerned with *what* the papers say than with *how* they say it.

Differences between the ways newspapers present their stories appear at even the most superficial level, the level which corresponds roughly with paralanguage in speech. First, there is the size of the page. The popular papers prefer a tabloid format which is approximately half the size of the broadsheet format preferred by the quality press. The two kinds of newspaper also favour different styles for their titles. The *Sun*, for example, has its title in white on a red background at the top left-hand corner of the page and the letters of 'The' are only a quarter the size of the 'S' in 'Sun'. The *Guardian*, however, prints its title in black letters. 'The' is in italics and 'Guardian' is emboldened, has an upper-case 'G' and is justified on the right-hand side of the paper. Headlines too usually contrast. Those in the quality papers offer a résumé of the story, such as 'End to martial law adds little to China's freedom', whereas those on the front page of the tabloids are often intended to intrigue or mystify: 'Pow! Prince caught with Batman's bird'. The different techniques are perhaps most apparent where the stories refer to the same incident. Both the *Guardian* and the *Sun* had an article on the expulsion of Father Ryan from the Order of Pallottine Fathers. The *Guardian* headlines it: 'Order expels Father Ryan' whereas the *Sun* prefers the more emotive 'Priests kick out IRA fugitive Ryan'.

Yet another difference at this paralinguistic level is the way the popular dailies vary the size and style of their print. The front page of the *Guardian* on 11 January had five different sizes of headline. The *Sun* had seven and, in addition, had three lines underlined and two in white on a black surface. It is possible that the solid blocks of print with which the quality papers confront their readers are judged too serious or unattractive for the kind of reader who prefers a paper which concentrates on simply expressed stories about sex, on gossip about celebrities and on extensive coverage of sport.

The level of grammar also exhibits interesting features. There is a tendency in all papers to avoid finite verbs in headlines, especially where the time reference is to the future. Thus, in the edition of the *Guardian* already referred to, we find the future indicated by means of the infinitive 'Hurd to put off Hong Kong reforms' and 'Britain to stick with Ferranti system for RAF's Euro-fighter'. The difficulties involved in making comprehensive generalisations about this aspect of language can, however, be illustrated by referring to another *Guardian* headline 'Kohl fears migration will hit East German economy' where the future is suggested by the use of the modal verb 'will'.

Contemporary time reference may be indicated in headlines by the simple present form. The *Guardian* and the *Sun* for 11 January supply such examples as 'Bank chief warns of loan rate rise', 'Ford offer undercuts pay policy', 'Di gets in shape at £500-a-night health farm' and 'Heavenly Bod Gail finds God'. The two papers differ in the frequency with which they use this form, however, the *Sun* often preferring to avoid verbs altogether 'Cecil's school for drunken drivers', 'Baby boom' and 'My problems by TV's Mr Problem'. Verbless headlines do, of course, appear in the *Guardian* as in 'Tunnel credit deadlock' but they form a much lower percentage. Both papers agree, on the other hand, in avoiding finite continuous forms of the verb.

Surprisingly, perhaps, in view of the fact that newspapers mainly report past events, explicit past time reference is relatively rare in headlines. Often the time reference is contemporary although the events themselves are clearly over: 'Prospectors win battle for Indian land' and 'Gulliver quits Broad Street with only a modest profit' from the *Guardian* and 'Jet dozer wakes in America' from the *Sun*. An equally common headline technique employed by the *Guardian* to refer to past events is the use of a past participle without an auxiliary as in 'Park-and-ride cut by BR' and 'Britain deadlocked in row over key EC posts'. The *Sun*, however, uses this form only slightly more often than it does the present participle constructions. And both newspapers tend to avoid finite, past tense forms.

Interesting grammatical differences are not, of course, confined to headlines. In introducing the people with whom a news story is concerned, the *Sun* likes to precede the name by a descriptive phrase, such as 'Wanted IRA terror priest Father Patrick Ryan', 'Round-the-world sailor John Paul', 'Cursing comic Dave Allen' and 'Ice-cool telly newsreader John Humphreys'. The *Guardian* favours a different technique, even in light-hearted stories. It often follows the name with a descriptive phrase as in 'Dr Mary Archer, scientist and immortally fragrant wife of the best-seller writer . . .' and 'Ayrton Senna, the 1988 world champion'.

The way public figures are referred to is also worthy of note. In the headlines, for example, the *Guardian* names British Ministers as 'Major', 'Hurd', 'Lamont' and 'Brooke'. The *Sun*, however, prefers 'Maggie' (Thatcher) and 'Cecil' (Parkinson). *Sun* stories, however, often preface the title with the job description, 'Prime Minister John Major' and 'Transport Secretary Malcolm Rifkind'. *Guardian* stories refer to him either as 'the Prime Minister' or as 'Mr Major'. It is a noticeable feature of the *Guardian*'s style of reference, indeed, that whereas the surname without a title is regularly used in headlines, the title plus the surname is invariable in the text, even when the reference is to a mass murderer. The *Sun*, by contrast, frequently relies on the first name alone, even in headlines.

Finally, newspaper language, and especially the language of headlines, has its own relatively exclusive set of vocabulary items. The 11 January, 1990 *Sun*, for example, includes such headlines as 'Payout Fury', 'Leftie in Jamaica fuss', 'Saucy gang nick sex goddess', 'City yuppie finds £4m in gutter', 'Divorce Dilemma', 'My nightmare is over' and 'Nash Trash'. The *Guardian* is less likely to use such vocabulary although the 11 January issue included 'Pace of reform brings clashes' and 'Senna faces ban threat'. Words such as 'ban', 'clash', 'crash', 'fury', 'horror', 'mob', 'pact', 'probe', 'rap', 'swindle' are a kind of journalistic shorthand, found mainly in newspaper headlines but occurring occasionally in news broadcasts.

Many adaptations of old words and coinages of new remain confined to the newspapers. Many also, however, make their way into our everyday vocabulary. It seems likely, for example, that newspapers first introduced us to 'Afro-American', 'bimbo', 'CFC gases', 'dinky' (double income no kids yet), 'ecology', 'gay', 'greens', 'hypothermia', 'identikit', 'unisex', 'yuppie' and 'zits'. Purists may object to such terms, usually on quite irrelevant grounds. The real objection to them may be that the uncritical adoption of such handy, ready-made words indicates a willingness to adopt ready-made thought and opinions. Perhaps our newspapers, instead of informing us, as is often claimed, are really doing our thinking for us. Most of us prefer to read the paper which we believe most closely reflects our own opinions. It may in fact be that we are reflecting theirs.

The account we have given here of the language of newspapers is, of course, incomplete. We have not been able to look, for example, at the way different topics such as finance, politics, sport or women's rights are treated in the same paper, or at the linguistic differences between articles and news reports. In addition, it could well have proved interesting to examine the ways local dailies like the *Yorkshire Post* differ from the nationals. Our research suggests that regional loyalties seem to overcome the class and education bias often reflected in the national newspapers. And there are many other aspects which could have been considered. But a really comprehensive account would fill a large book. All we have available here is part of a chapter and so we have had to limit ourselves to a brief sketch supported by a few illustrative examples showing the kind of features that a more complete description would have to account for.

We turn now to a more recently developed but no less influential medium: the radio.

From 1926 onwards radio broadcasts began to be received in an ever-increasing number of homes and, for the first time in history, it became possible for one person to be heard simultaneously by thousands, and eventually millions, throughout the entire country. These voices which spoke from London had an unenviable responsibility thrust upon them, because most of the people who listened to them assumed that they were hearing the authentic sound of perfectly spoken English.

Those who were in control of the new medium recognised and accepted this responsibility. However, because a standard written form of English was already in widespread use, particularly in the sphere of education, they saw that responsibility as being much more concerned with pronunciation than with grammar or vocabulary. Thus is was that the Director of the British Broadcasting Company (later Corporation), J. C. W. Reith, who was himself a Scot with a recognisably Scottish accent, set up a committee in 1926 to inquire into the pronunciation to be used by announcers. He expounded his own attitude to broadcast English two years later, in 1928, in the following terms:

Since the earliest days of broadcasting the BBC has recognised a great responsibility towards the problems of spoken English. These are vexed but intriguing. They might have been evaded, leaving both general principles and particular words to chance. Tendencies might have been observed and either reinforced or resisted. As the broadcaster is influential, so also is he open to criticism from every quarter in that he addresses listeners of every degree of education, many of whom are influenced by local vernacular and tradition. There has been no attempt to establish a uniform spoken language, but it seemed desirable to adopt uniformity of principle and uniformity of pronunciation to be observed by Announcers with respect to doubtful words. The policy might be described as that of seeking a common denominator of educated speech.

The 'common denominator' pronunciation that was adopted was RP (see Chapter 2) and people throughout Britain, most of whom would otherwise have little contact with this accent, began to hear it regularly and to be influenced by it, both in their own practice and in their attitude to other accents.

The committee on pronunciation set up by Reith was headed by a phonetician, A. Lloyd James. He made his own views on the subject public in 1931 when he made the following claims:

(1)   There are distinct variants of speech in every social class, and class variants in every district.
(2)   Local variants become increasingly unlike one another as we descend the social scale.
(3)   They become more alike as we ascend.
(4)   The greater mobility of educated people tends towards the elimination of some of their local peculiarities.
(5)   The general spread of education tends to bring about the unification of the social variants in all districts.
(6)   Out of the broad band that comprises all district and class variants, there is emerging a considerably narrower band of variants that have a very great measure of similarity.
(7)   This narrow band of types has more features in common with Southern English than with Northern English.
(8)   Those who speak any one variety of the narrow band are recognised as educated speakers throughout the country. They may broadcast without fear of adverse intelligent criticism.

The terms of Lloyd James's remarks unfortunately obscure the very important distinction between a socio-regional dialect of English on the one hand and Standard English spoken with a socio-regional accent on the other: a confusion that is still so widespread that anyone who speaks with a local accent is usually thought to be speaking a dialect.

The distinction had never before mattered a great deal. The need for a standard language had been felt, and met, in writing, but, previously, the question of a standard pronunciation had not arisen. It was raised now by the advent of this new, spoken mass medium. The problem Lloyd James was really addressing himself to was this: given a standard grammar and vocabulary, but no standard pronunciation, what can be done to ensure uniformity in spoken English? Although he failed to pose the question in these exact terms, there is no doubt about his answer. The variety of local accents would be replaced by the one non-local accent, namely, RP. In effect, what he was arguing for in the remarks quoted above was that all broadcasters should sound like him and use the pronunciation he had, no doubt, been required to adopt as part of his own initiation into the educated elite of his day.

Thus it was that RP came to be closely associated with the BBC, so closely associated, indeed, that English spoken in this accent became popularly known as 'BBC English'. And the association has endured because, although other kinds of English are now more frequently heard than was once the case, the voice of authority on the radio still prefers RP. An occasional disc jockey, trade union official, gardening expert or sporting celebrity may be permitted to address the public in a more demotic accent, but the news and official announcements are still read in RP. And when the standard seems to be slipping, the public is quick to criticise and complain.

Although it was not accorded the same degree of conscious attention as pronunciation, grammar was an important element in broadcast English. It provided an increasingly familiar standard for all sections of the community and, in this way, augmented the influence of education in establishing in the popular mind the notion of a 'correct' English. When broadcasting began, the normal speech of most of the community was some form of dialect. Standard English was encountered in school or church, for those who attended these institutions, but more interaction at work and at play was conducted in dialect. Although aware of Standard English, therefore, the ordinary citizen felt little obligation to acquire or imitate it. Then came the radio, bringing Standard English into every home. Probably for the first time in history, dialect speakers began to feel not just that their language was 'different' but that it was in some way 'wrong'. This, possibly unconscious, feeling has undoubtedly been a powerful factor, although by no means the only one, in the gradual modification of both the pronunciation and grammar of dialect speech. A total transformation of regional pronunciation in the direction of RP was impossible, but local accents are undeniably less 'broad' than they were. The grammar of the radio, however, proved less hard to adopt.

The adoption of a standard grammar does not remove either the necessity for, or the possibility of, stylistic variation. Radio news reports, for example, have developed a style appropriate to a speech situation in which information has to be given clearly and comprehensively in a strictly limited period of time. Nor has the addressee the opportunity to question the speakers or slow them down in any way if what is said is not immediately understood. Newspaper readers can read and re-read any complicated passages until the meaning is clear but radio listeners are rarely given a second chance. What is not understood at once is probably not understood at all. Radio news bulletins, therefore, commonly consist of only a small number of items, to each of which is allotted a few, structurally uncomplicated, sentences. The following, taken from BBC Radio Leeds at 10:00 on a morning in February, 1990, is a fairly typical example:

> Reports are coming in of an air-crash in the southern Indian city of Bangalore. Reports are still sketchy but officials at the airport say over a hundred passengers who were on the Indian Airlines internal flight have been killed. Thirty-five of those on board are thought to have survived. Mark Tully reports from Delhi:

> The A320 Airbus with a hundred and forty-two people on board was on a scheduled flight of Indian Airlines, the internal carrier, from Bombay to Bangalore. It crashed some 4000 feet short of the runway at Bangalore Airport in the middle of the day. The Airbus is fitted with the latest avionics and was only introduced by Indian Airlines last year. It's made by Airbus Industry in which British Aerospace have a 20 per cent holding. They manufacture the wings. Indian Airlines pilots had earlier expressed reservations about the difficulties in maintaining such an advanced aircraft in this country. A pilot of an Airbus ran into severe difficulties when a bird crashed into it over Delhi Airport last year.

The same item is handled rather differently on two other BBC news programmes the same morning. At 10:30, Radio 1 announced:

> An Indian airliner has crashed as it came in to land at the southern city of Bangalore. It's feared that more than a hundred people have been killed. We've just had this report from Mark Tully:

> The A330 Airbus was on a scheduled flight of Indian Airlines, the internal carrier, from Bombay to Bangalore. It crashed less than a hundred yards short of the perimeter of Bangalore Airport in the middle of the day. One report says that more than a hundred and fifty people have been killed and that there were a few survivors. As an Indian Airline spokesman has said, there were only one hundred and forty-two people on board. The Airbus is fitted with the latest computerised controls and was only brought into service by Indian Airlines last year. It's made by Airbus Industry in which British Aerospace have a 20 per cent holding. They manufacture the wings. Indian Airline pilots had earlier expressed reservations about the difficulties of maintaining such an advanced aircraft in this country.

At 12:00, Radio 4 produced a much shorter account and did not introduce a report from Mark Tully or any other 'on-the-spot' reporter:

A European Airbus A320 airliner operated by India Airlines has crashed on landing at the southern city of Bangalore. The plane, on a scheduled flight from Bombay, came down short of the runway. About one hundred and fifty people are said to have been on board and there are reports of some survivors. One spokesman has put the figure at fifty.

What is most noticeable about these reports is the variation to be found at the levels of both content and form. In the Radio 4 report, the Airbus is an A320; on Radio 1 it is an A330. The crash is described as happening 'some 4000 feet short of the runway', 'less than a hundred yards short of the perimeter' and 'short of the runway'. The numbers of passengers and survivors differ too, with Mark Tully giving a precise number of passengers and Radio 4 preferring an approximation attributed to an unnamed spokesman 'About one hundred and fifty people are said to have been on board'. It is, of course, extremely difficult to get precise information on any disaster and Mark Tully was reporting from Delhi, not Bangalore.

The form of the items also differs. Radio Leeds and Radio 1 both chose to have a report within a report. Radio 4 preferred an uninterrupted four-sentence statement. Radio Leeds suggests the immediacy of their coverage by their verb choices 'are coming in', 'are still sketchy' and 'are thought'. Radio 1 cultivates a more intimate style with the use of contractions in the announcement 'It's feared' and 'We've just had'. Radio 4 script-writers are the most formal. They have also had more time to package the information. It will be noticed that each sentence is constructed to give maximum information; that they do not say that anyone was killed although they imply as much; that their attributions are all non-specific 'About one hundred and fifty people are said' and 'One spokesman'; and that there is no speculation about what caused the crash.

So far as grammar is concerned, stylistic variation usually keeps within the limits of the standard language. A sports commentary style will often, for example, favour short, simple sentences, whereas the narrative of more formal occasions permits greater variety of structure. A commentary on a royal event, for example, is more consciously precise than a description of a miners' gala in Durham, although both, in contrast to football commentating, are likely to report a contemporary action using the progressive: 'Her Majesty is walking slowly down between the two lines of dignitaries'; 'The first marchers are now passing the Town Hall'. But whatever the form chosen, it will be within the possibilities offered by the standard language. Flexibility in contextual application is one thing but novelty of form quite another.

Vocabulary usage is different. At this level broadcast English readily accepts innovation and can even be said to encourage it in such fields as popular music. It is easy to criticise the ephemeral nature of such items as 'funky', 'groovy', 'way out' and 'with it' but, on the other hand, what can we now call a 'disc jockey' if we eschew this term? And who still calls a 'record-player' or 'stereo' a 'gramophone'? 'Popular music' has, of course become 'pop music' and then simply 'pop' and this abbreviation has itself become productive in the language, giving us such formations as 'pop art', 'pop charts', 'pop opera', 'pop star' and even 'pop culture', a phrase which some speakers might regard as internally contradictory.

Nor is innovation confined to the field of popular music. Purists often complain about the tendency of the radio, and especially Radio 1, to popularise Americanisms such as 'to ad-lib', 'sexy' or 'hopefully' in such a sentence as 'Hopefully, the fire is now out'. Perhaps a better-grounded complaint could be directed against the infiltration of non-musical views and opinions on the part of some of the disc jockeys, together with an apparent indifference to the precise use of language. Over the last year, for example, we have recorded 'less people' instead of 'fewer people', 'have showed' instead of 'have shown', 'educationalists' instead of 'educationists' and 'enormity' to mean size rather than seriousness.

In some ways, the developments in radio have replicated the patterning of the newspapers. With the exploitation of cheap transistors in the 1950s, radio costs fell and the number of available channels proliferated. Today, radio listeners may tune in to the BBC or commercial radio, the latter paying for itself by means of selling advertising. Both the BBC and commercial radio are subdivided into national and regional stations, although the strength of commercial radio tends to lie in its strong regional appeal.

Nationally, the BBC has five broadcasting channels, Radios 1, 2, 3, 4 and 5. These, like the newspapers, attract different sections of society with Radios 1, 2 and 5 having some of the appeal of tabloids and Radios 3 and 4 being closer to the qualities. A brief sample of the broadcasts for one day indicates the differences. Radios 1 and 2 are almost exclusively popular music, chat, news, competitions and phone-ins, with Radio 2 attracting an older group of listeners; Radio 3 appeals unashamedly to the lover of classical music and Radio 4 attempts to be an omnipurpose channel providing news and comment, consumer programmes, plays and book-reading as well as a number of topics related to religion, handicrafts and hobbies.

It is not always easy to separate radio from television in terms of their effect on the English language. There are some differences, however. In particular, while radio has tended to remain an influence at the nation level, television has developed into a powerful international force. The cost of mounting a television programme can be enormous (a thirty-second television commercial for a nationally known product, for example, has been known to cost half a million pounds). This means that television producers have to be internationally minded in order to sell their programmes abroad and, by the same token, national television services have to make use of a great many foreign imports.

Television, therefore, has greatly extended the process of making everyone familiar with different varieties of English and a wider range of experience. No longer are children exposed only to the speech of their region and class. Almost all children in Britain are as familiar with the speech of the *Neighbours* of Ramsey Street, Australia, or of the characters of *Sesame Street* as they are with that of their parents. And older children are as likely to reflect the speech patterns of a favourite pop star as those of their relatives or friends. Children are also exposed to televised versions of films made for their parents' or even grandparents' generation and so are often able to share in the linguistic experiences of their elders. It is not unusual to see a child-mimic reproducing James Cagney's facial expressions to the accompaniment of 'You dirty rat!' or to have several generations in a family respond in similar ways to the catch-phrase 'Play it again, Sam', which has been inaccurately attributed to Humphrey Bogart. Radio and television are thus extending the experience, both linguistic and non-linguistic, of everyone in the speech community.

As a result of all that they see and hear on television, people have generally become much more conscious of language, of the power it has and of the status associated with certain varieties. At the same time there has been a growth of scepticism and mistrust in what is said by those with political power. Thus, there has developed what is sometimes called a 'credibility gap' between the community and its leaders, who no longer automatically enjoy the prestige and admiration to which their success might once have entitled them.

It is tempting to believe that this means people are becoming more discerning, more capable of recognising truth. All that has really happened, however, is that the intimacy of the television medium has made it less easy for politicians to lie convincingly, or to conceal their ordinariness from the public. And, unfortunately, our awareness of the power of language has not made us any more sensitive to it, because trust in personalities has often been replaced by trust in slogans and cliches. As a consequence, politicians have learnt to seek the help of advertising agencies, and to promote themselves using the same marketing skills that sell washing powders and cornflakes. The 1987 election slogans 'Labour talk. We deliver.' and 'The Tories say unemployment is falling. (It must be election time again.)' offered little more intellectual challenge than 'Go to work on an egg'. However, such highly publicised slogans have become essential to the political packaging of today.

Packaging is not, of course, limited to advertising and politics. Television news programmes, which are the primary source of daily news in Britain, have also been designed as media formats which must entertain as well as inform. News broadcasts are often structures in a framework such as:

News signature tune and moving logo
Male overvoice announcing the edition (e.g. News at One)
Introduction of newscasters
Summary of two to five main headlines
Report on each item, usually involving headline, story outline, on-the-spot correspondents, reactions (often from politicians from different parties) and implications
Half-way summary
News items often with an amusing 'And finally'
Conclusion, often equating the bulletin with the news itself: 'And that's the national and international news for tonight'.

Quotations within the bulletin may be attributed ('The Prime Minister announced') or unattributed ('A statement from Downing Street'), direct ('We must not give in to threats') or indirect (that they [or 'we'] should not give in to threats). The verbs of attribution used by broadcasters can be neutral ('said', 'commented', 'added'), negative ('accused', 'admitted', 'demanded') or positive ('assured', 'encouraged', 'emphasised') and, since reported speech occupies approximately 20 per cent of television news talk, attributive verbs, with or without modification ('angrily', 'quietly', 'for the tenth time') can create an impression of power, success or failure. This impression is often reinforced by the 'sound bite' or short section of speech selected to be shown on the news. Increasingly, news editors go for the short, pithy utterance and increasingly that is exactly what well-trained politicians provide.

Film, like television, is a visual medium as well as an aural one, but it is neither so intimate nor so immediate in its impact.

It has been claimed by Marckwardt and Quirk (1964) that British cinema-goers at first found the accent and idiom of American films difficult to understand. With regard to accents, however, it is not clear why British audiences should have had much more trouble than American ones. Certainly, few people in Britain travelled much in the 1920s, and fewer still travelled far, with the result that their exposure to regional and social language variety must have been limited. The 1914–18 war, however, had undoubtedly resulted in the weakening of British class barriers and Britain was still the centre of an enormous trading empire which sent people from all regions and classes to distant parts of the globe. The British were not all that parochial in comparison with the Americans, therefore, although the latter have traditionally been regarded as much more mobile, both regionally and socially. In addition, American films were, from the start, hospitable to a variety of accents, including British ones. Their stars came from many different parts of the world, not only the English-speaking world, and little attempt was made to modify or standardise the accents they brought with them. Some at least must have been unfamiliar to American ears too.

Undoubtedly, however, American accents did predominate, and a number of British actors (Cary Grant and Greer Garson, for example) even developed what is sometimes called a 'mid-Atlantic' pronunciation, thus concealing their origins. And the range of American pronunciations represented was certainly wide, whereas British representation was mainly confined to RP. As a result, it is probably true to say that British film-goers became familiar with a greater variety of American pronunciation than was true in the opposite direction. Even today there are many British accents which Americans find difficult to understand, but there are few American ones which give any trouble to the British.

Accent variety was not merely incidental in American films, however; it could be functional, too. It was and, to a lesser extent, still is one of the primary devices used to create stereotypes. A southern Irish accent, for example, is almost invariably associated with a large, well-meaning, loyal dunderhead who enjoys a drink and a fight; a German accent often signals humourless intelligence; a French accent is romantic; a Mexican one either funny or sinister, depending on whether the character carries a guitar or a rifle. American Blacks were for many years portrayed as stupid and feckless, a stereotype that was signalled by a 'Yessum-Mister-Tom-a's-a-comin' pronunciation which moulded and confirmed popular prejudices a great deal more effectively than any Ku Klux Klan propaganda. 'Normal' people, of course, spoke 'American'.

Grammar can also be useful for stereotyping. In general, the grammar used in films is that of the standard language. Like eighteenth- and nineteenth-century novelists, film directors are likely to idealise the linguistic performance of their main characters. Non-standard forms like 'She ain't in' or 'He never said nothin' to me' are permitted to servants and minor characters, but the main performers generally speak Standard English, regardless of their social or regional origins. Even Tarzan, to whom Hollywood and not Edgar Rice Burroughs gave the immortal line 'Me Tarzan, you Jane', spoke Standard English most of the time. In recognition of the strangeness of his upbringing and background, however, he was denied the use of reduced forms such as 'I'm', 'you're', 'isn't' and 'didn't'. Aliens from space or from lost continents are likely to suffer a similar grammatical deprivation.

The grammar of film language, therefore, rarely presented any problems to English-speaking film-goers, although they may have experienced some initial difficulties with vocabulary. Thus, in films, they encountered, probably for the first time, 'corrals', 'round-ups', 'showdowns', 'boot-leggers', 'speakeasies', 'the Mafia', 'the electric chair', 'private eyes', 'cops', 'stir' and 'screws', for example. Many of these items remained passive, heard only in the cinema and rarely used productively except by children acting out their fantasies. American films have, however, either introduced or popularised a large number of expressions which have acquired wider usage, though seldom to the extent of being accepted into

Standard English. Most people, at some time or other, have used or encountered the following in conversation: 'clip-joint', 'creep', 'dough' (i.e. money), 'dude', 'going straight', '(tough) guys', 'heel', 'hick', 'hill-billy', 'hoodlum', 'hooked' (on drugs), 'joint' (as in 'strip-joint' and, more recently, in connection with drugs), 'ragtime', 'rocks' (i.e. jewels), 'on the run', 'smashed', 'stoned' and 'yellow'. And we all know what is meant by 'cut it out', 'hit the trail' or 'he got a sock on the jaw'. A little thought will extend the list considerably. We are not, of course, recommending the use of such expressions, but merely commenting on their existence. They are neither better nor worse for having been introduced into the language through the medium of films.

Nowadays, as we have suggested, the influence of films tends to mingle with that of television. Most films eventually end up on the small screen; successful television series are often made into films; and popular films can give rise to even more popular television series. But it is doubtful whether films have more than a marginal influence in the context of television and, apart from their appearance on television, they probably have much less effect on our thinking and behaviour, including our language behaviour, than was formerly the case.

As for the future, although all the media will no doubt play some part, television and radio will probably prove to be the most powerful influences as far as English is concerned. Such influence may not always be for the good. There are many, for example, who believe that reliance on television, and to a lesser extent radio, will have a detrimental effect on the teaching of literacy. It could also be argued that both broadcasting media, because of their continual searching after novelty in language, especially obvious in pop music broadcasts aimed at the young, and in advertising, distort and trivialise the language. But against such negative effects can be set many positive ones. Television and radio do widen horizons for all of us and bring experiences and information to the masses which were, until recently, reserved for the few.

Nor does it seem likely that the language's role as an international lingua franca will be adversely affected by the influence of the media. Today, English is the official or most widely used language in more countries than any other world language, being spoken in some form by close to one thousand million people. It is improbable that this situation will be radically changed in the immediate future because there are, and will continue to be, pressures at work to preserve the inter-intelligibility of international Englishes.

On 20 June, 1978, Dr Robert Burchfield, Chief Editor of the *Oxford English Dictionary*, gave a lecture in Chicago in which he suggested that British and American varieties are continuing to move apart and that they will become increasingly dissimilar in spite of the power of the media. Later, on 30 July, 1978, in an article in the *Observer*, he explained this view by listing a number of expressions like 'to badmouth' (i.e. to malign), 'boonies' (isolated region), 'to schlepp' (drag, pull) which would not be widely understood in Britain. It is perfectly true that many lexical items from the States are unfamiliar in Britain though some of Burchfield's examples are unfortunate. 'Badmouthing' is familiar to Britons with West Indian connections and 'schlepp' is quite widely used in Yiddish-influenced circles in Britain and South Africa as well as in America. One must add, however, that such lexical and idiomatic differences could be highlighted from any two varieties of English, including two British varieties. Many people in England, for example, would be confused by such Northern Ireland expressions as: 'big-headed' (forgetful), 'thickwitted' (stubborn), 'annoyed' (very worried), 'astray in the head' (worried sick), 'bold' (naughty), 'I've got the founder' (I've caught a bad cold), 'he's got a long finger on him' (he's inclined to steal), 'you've quare hands on you' (you're a gifted workman); and we have limited our examples to phrases involving English-derived items, although such Gaelic-influenced expressions as 'a wee shannach' (a friendly chat), 'a ceileyin' match' (an evening visit which is friendly and lively) and 'a bit flahool' (overgenerous) would be even less widely understood.

Nevertheless, the existence of such forms does not preclude understanding between English people and speakers from Northern Ireland largely because no Northern Ireland speaker would use such expressions in conversation with a stranger. They are part of a colloquial style that would be used only with intimates. It seems to us, therefore, that listing vocabulary items or phrases which are limited to one regional area or to one group is not an indication that varieties are diverging. Rather, it is merely acknowledging the fact that one variety of a language may lack the means of describing some of the ethnic and cultural associations of another group of people. Unless and until a 1984-type society arises and human beings become undifferentiated automatons, the need for expressing individuality, for marking intimacy, for creative expression, will ensure that differences will occur in English, differences which will mark out the young from the old, the socially fortunate from the deprived. But it seems likely to us that these differences will increasingly be restricted to differences of pronunciation or of style within a standard framework rather than to new or widely different varieties of language. Even Citizen Band (CB) which many commentators assumed was a new dialect is really only a stylistic modification of English.

Although computers are not, strictly speaking, a mass medium, their increased use over the last decade has influenced English in a number of ways. The first and most obvious influence is in the new meanings that have been given to words. A 'mouse' is no longer a rodent but a small gadget to speed up commands; a 'chip' is an integrated system and a 'bug' is either a mistake in the 'software' (i.e. programs) or a malfunction in the 'hardware' (the physical components of the computer). Secondly, there is widespread use of abbreviations, blends and acronyms. A dot matrix printer is a DMP;

a personal computer is a PC; a 'bit' is a *bi*nary digi*t*, 'pixels' are picture (*<pics*) *el*ements; WIMPS are *w*indows, *i*cons, *m*ice and *p*ointers and BASIC is Beginners All-Purpose Symbolic Instruction Code. Thirdly, American spellings are used in words such as 'analog', 'disk' and 'program', resulting in a form of specialisation where the British spelling continues to be used for all the meanings of the words outside the field of computers. And lastly, computerese (computer jargon) is affecting the speech of people who have never used computers. When politicians talk about 'interfacing' with particular people, for example, they are using the word in its computer sense of 'having a shared boundary' and when a person of limited imagination is described as having 'read only memory' or ROM, the metaphor comes from computers.

It seems to us that the strong prestige of the standard language allied to its continued use in education and in the media, especially television, will ensure that Standard English will remain an international lingua franca and that extreme divergences will not be tolerated. United States English will not in the foreseeable future become a different language from British English although international English may increasingly be modelled on the former since, apart from its military and economic strength, the United States has more than four times as many native speakers as Britain.

In summing up, we should like to stress a number of points. First, the media are interactive. Not only do they influence each other, but they often offer a summary, preview or commentary on each other. Thus Radio 4 has a daily report: 'What the papers say'; each daily newspaper surveys the programmes on radio and television; and newspaper critics often assume the responsibility of correcting mistakes or misrepresentations that occur in the broadcasting media.

Secondly, the media have different strengths. Radio and television can offer instantaneous coverage of an event – an air disaster, a kidnapping, a freak storm, the falling to earth of a satellite – but the press alone can offer extensive explanation and amplification of such occurrences. Newspapers, by providing comprehensive coverage of complex issues, can thus complement the more immediate reports of radio and television. Films are probably less influential now than they were before televisions became standard equipment in most households. Yet the size of its screen and the fact that film-goers must make a conscious decision to go to the cinema ensure that their role of providing spectacle and entertainment is still of considerable importance.

Finally, our intention in this chap.₋r has been to deal with the interaction between language and the media, but neither language nor the media are constants, and so our comments are intended as useful insights rather than as a definitive guide. We have focused on some of the major linguistic usages associated with each medium and suggested certain ways in which readers may continue their own exploration of the language of the media.

Additional Reading

Ang, I. (1985), *Watching Dallas: Soap Opera and the Melodramatic Imagination* (London: Routledge).

Armes, R. (1988), *On Video* (London: Routledge).

Atkinson, M. (1984), *Our Masters' Voices: The Language and Body-language of Politics* (London: Routledge).

Baistow, T. (1985), *The Fourth-rate Estate: An Anatomy of Fleet Street* (London: Routledge).

Bordwell, D., Staiger, J. and Thompson, K. (1988), *The Classical Hollywood Cinema* (London: Routledge).

Boyd-Barrett, O. and Braham, P. (1986), *Media, Knowledge and Power* (London: Routledge).

Briggs, A. (1961–5), *The History of Broadcasting in the United Kingdom*, 3 vols (Oxford: Oxford University Press).

Burchfield, R. et al. (1979), *The Quality of Spoken English on BBC Radio* (London: BBC Publications).

Cohen, S. and Yong, J. (eds) (1973), *The Manufacture of News* (London: Constable).

Crissell, Andrew (1986), *Understanding Radio* (London: Routledge).

Crystal, D. and Davy, D. (1969), *Investigating English Style* (London: Longmans).

Curran, J. and Seaton, J. (1988), *Power Without Responsibility: The Press and Broadcasting in Britain* (London: Routledge).

Curran, J., Smith, A. and Wingate, P. (1987), *Impacts and Influences: Media Power in the Twentieth Century* (London: Routledge).

Davis, H. and Walton, P. (1983), *Language, Image, Media* Oxford: Blackwell).

Day, R. (1976), *Day to Day* (London: W. Kimber and Co.).

Derbyshire, I. (1988), *Politics in Britain* Edinburgh: Chambers).

Dimbleby, R. and Burton, G. (1985), *More than Words: An Introduction to Communication* (London: Routledge).

Dunnett, P. (1987), *The World Newspaper Industry* (London: Routledge).

Eisenstein, S. (1959), *Notes of a Film Director* (London: Lawrence and Wishart).

Eysenck, H. J. and Nias, D. K. B. (1978), *Sex, Violence and the Media* (London: Temple Smith).

Fiske, J. (1987), *Television Culture* (London: Routledge).

Geis, M. L. (1984), *The Language of Television Advertising* (London: Academic Press).

Glasgow University Media Group (1976/1980), *Bad News/More Bad News* (London: Routledge and Kegan Paul).

Golding, P. and Elliott, P. (1979), *Making the News* (London: Longman).

Harrison, M. (1985), *TV News: Whose Bias?* (London: Policy Journals).

Hartley, J. (1982), *Understanding News* (London: Methuen).

Karpf, A. (1988), *Doctoring the Media: The Reporting of Health and Medicine* (London: Routledge).

Kerr, P. (1986), *The Hollywood Film Industry* (London: Routledge).

Kilborn, R. (1986), *The Multi-Media Melting Pot* (London: Routledge).

Kingsley, H. (1988), *Soap Box* (London: Macmillan).

Marckwardt, A. H. and Quirk, R. (1964), *British and American English* (Voice of America and BBC).

McCrum, R. et al. (1986), *The Story of English* (London: Faber and Faber and BBC Publications).

McLuhan, M. (1987), *Understanding Media* (London: Ark Paperback).

Morley, D. (1987), *Family Television* (London: Routledge).

Negrine, R. (1989), *Politics and the Mass Media in Britain* (London: Routledge).

Quicke, A. (1976), *Tomorrow's Television* (London: Lion Books).

Richards, J. and Sheridan, D. (1987), *Mass Observation at the Movies* (London: Routledge).

Richards, J. (1989), *The Age of the Dream Palace* (London: Routledge).

Schlesinger, P. (1987), *Putting 'Reality' Together* (London: Routledge).

Smith, M. and Miles, P. (1987), *Cinema, Literature and Society* (London: Routledge).

Spiegl, F. (1983), *Keep Taking the Tabloids* (London: Pan).

Stead, P. (1989), *Film and the Working Class* (London: Routledge).

Tyrrell, R. (1977), *The Work of the Television Journalist* (London: Focal Press).

Waddington, D., Jones, K. and Critcher, C. (1989), *Flashpoints: Studies in Public Disorder* (London: Routledge).

Whitaker, B. (1985), *News Ltd: Why You Can't Read All About It* (London: Routledge).

Whitaker, B. and Morley, D. (1986), *The Press, Radio and Television* (London: Routledge).

Williams, R. (1990), *Television* (London: Routledge).

6 English in Advertising

In the previous chapter we examined the interaction between language and the media. We saw how interrelated the media are and how they influence one another and the speech community. We now wish to deal with advertising, a form of persuasion which is directed at large numbers of people by means of the media. Advertising, for example, accounts for almost a third of the space in our daily newspapers and for approximately a tenth of the viewing time of ITV, Channel 4 and the satellite television channels, BSkyB (British Sky Broadcasting). Many local radio stations are totally dependent on advertising revenue and it is becoming increasingly difficult to take an outing without being reminded that Guinness is 'Pure Genius' or 'Once driven, forever smitten'.

Advertising is a complex phenomenon because it involves two inter-acting processes, namely, communication and persuasion, and both processes are many-faceted. To get some idea of the complexity of an advertisement, the reader might begin by asking the questions: who says what? to whom? by what means? and to what effect? The answers will show that language is only one strand in the communication network and that, under the guise of straightforward simplicity, advertisements are usually subtle and carefully structured.

It may be useful at this stage to make a distinction between the so-called 'hard-sell' and 'soft-sell' approaches to advertising. The hard-sell technique is relatively straightforward. It urges the consumer to buy a particular product and offers one or more 'reasons' why this particular product should be bought. At its crudest level, the hard-sell line is 'Buy Brand X because it is cheapest and best'. The soft-sell approach uses more subtle and indirect methods. Perhaps a beautiful girl appears on the television screen. She catches every eye; all the men admire; all the women envy; and it is suggested, all because the girl uses a certain hairspray or deodorant or gets her clothes from a particular chain store.

Detergents are utilitarian products which have, traditionally, been presented by means of a hard-sell approach; chocolates, on the other hand, are luxury items and are often associated in advertisements with promises of romance, wish-fulfilment or merely a taste of paradise. The former technique often goes with bold typography, uncomplicated copy like

'Brand X adds softness to cleanness and whiteness' and relatively uninteresting visuals. Soft-sell advertising, however, appeals to the emotions and tries to establish a link between a product and beauty or wealth, romance or self-confidence, success or prestige. Advertisements for a well-known brand of chocolates, for example, imply that a man will perform extraordinary feats of daring such as swinging across Manhattan on a crane 'And all because the lady loves Milk Tray'.

A close scrutiny of recent advertisements suggests that, as far as national advertising is concerned, it is the soft-sell technique which is now most popular. Local advertisers, it appears, cannot afford the time or the money to create a brand image and so they still use such copy as 'Don't miss our double discount sale', but national advertisements, even when promoting detergents, now favour a more emotive, less direct approach. Their aim seems to be to gain and maintain group loyalty to one brand. And in a world where there is often no genuine or rational reason for preferring one brand to another, the soft-sell approach seems more appropriate. As far as detergents are concerned, the advertisement is normally aimed at women and there is a strong suggestion that happy, successful women owe at least part of their contentment to their washing powder.

Many advertisers study their target audiences closely in an attempt to create the image and message most likely to influence behaviour. In the past, this was done mainly by classifying consumers according to the six main sociological groups: A = upper class, B = upper middle, C_1 = lower middle, C_2 = skilled workers, D = unskilled workers and E = people on fixed incomes. Since money tends to circulate most freely among C_2, D and E, most popular advertisements were aimed at the people in these groups. More recently, psychological profiles have been used. Expressing this point a lot more simplistically than most advertisers do, we can suggest that consumers can also be thought of as Mainstreamers, Aspirers, Succeeders and Reformers.

Mainstreamers, making up perhaps 40 per cent of the population, need security. They prefer to buy food in a few reputable stores (such as Marks and Spencer or Sainsbury); they go mainly for brandnames; tend to buy Ford cars and are security conscious. Aspirers need status symbols. They use cash cards, read the most recent magazines, play squash or an equivalent and are the buyers of the current success symbols. Succeeders are often over 40 and do not feel the need for status symbols. They like to be in control and are in the market for services, such as financial advice, rather than goods. Reformers are often teachers and journalists, readers of the *Guardian* or the *Independent*. They are more interested in the 'quality of life' than in possessions. They take a positive stance on ecology, the Third World, Nuclear Disarmament and go for 'natural' products such as pine furniture. They often buy 'own label' goods in a store, except for catfood, where they go for an expensive brandname.

Most of us belong to one or more of the above groups. We all value our individuality; we want to be different but not too different. Advertisers study the profiles of buyers and are increasingly adept at matching products and markets. Although popular advertisements for cereals and detergents, for example, are still aimed at a mass audience, others, such as those for holidays or retirement homes, are being directed at specially targeted groups such as the well-off, older people sometimes called 'woopies'.

It seems reasonable to suggest that people are not necessarily persuaded to buy an object or to behave in a particular way by a linguistic appeal to logic. On the contrary, advertising often appeals to such psychological universals as greed, envy or fear, although consumers may not be directly aware of the pressures to which they are being subjected. It would appear, too, that the prestige of the communicator is an important factor in the success of advertising. Otherwise, Frank Bruno would not be used to recommend a sauce, without which he is not 'HP' (happy). Nor would well-known television stars such as Diane Keen and Sharon Maughan be asked to laud the virtues of instant coffees. Evidently, the advertisers hope that some of the prestige associated with the communicator of the message will be transferred to their product.

The aim of the advertiser is quite specific. He wishes to capture the attention of the members of the mass audience and by means of a short message – often verbal but sometimes visual – persuade them to buy a product or behave in a particular way, such as going to Cooks for all their holiday needs. We do not intend to examine the psychological aspects of advertising or the influence of such non-linguistic phenomena as colour, music, visual displays or the communicator's rapport with the audience. Instead, although it is only one of the elements contributing to the extraordinary effects of advertising, we shall restrict our discussion to the language component.

As we have said, advertising exploits all the media and, to the casual observer, the techniques employed for radio, television and films may appear radically different from those appearing in a written medium. Detailed examination of advertising copy, however, suggests that such expectations are rarely fulfilled. In advertising language the distinctions usually found in speech and writing are blurred. This blurring seems to be caused by three main factors. First, the language of all advertising is apparently simple, and is often based on colloquial speech:

Have a break. Have a Kitkat.

Once you've tasted Danish, nothing else will do.

Secondly, all advertising copy is written. Often indeed the simplest, most spontaneous-sounding advertisements are clearly the result not only of ingenuity but also of reflection. The colloquial impression of

Get the Max. Get the taste.

is belied by the parallelism of the two imperatives and by the punning on 'Max', an abbreviation suggesting both Maxwell House coffee and maximum appeal. And thirdly, there is much inter-influencing from radio to magazine, from television to poster. It is quite usual for a major advertising campaign to make use of several media. A product may be introduced on television, given wide coverage in colour supplements and then further impressed on people's minds by means of posters. Schweppes, for example, made a series of television commercials based on the sound 'sh' and Schweppes' agents were subsequently able to advertise their product, even on buses, merely by the use of 'Sch . . .'.

The main aim of all advertising is to familiarise consumers with the benefits of particular products in the hope of increasing sales, and the techniques used by advertisers do not vary markedly. A poster is often merely glimpsed in passing and so, to be effective, its message must be colourful, legible, understandable and memorable. The rules governing the language of other types of advertising are similar. We shall now examine some advertising copy to show what we mean.

The language of advertising often appears simple because of its fondness for short sentences:

After 5 p.m. a Big Mac is only 99p.

Thank Halfords for that.

and because co-ordination is preferred to subordination:

You can't improve on a Mars. But you can improve on ice-cream. (Mars ice-cream bar)

Caravanning. Get up and go.

Marks and says a lot about you. (Marks and Spencer)

Passives are avoided and the vocabulary tends to be drawn from everyday, colloquial language. Monosyllabic words far outnumber polysyllabic ones and many brand names, too, have one syllable: 'Bloo', 'Bold', 'Breeze', 'Daz', 'Fab', 'Haig', 'Jif', 'Shield', 'Stork', 'Surf'. However, since 'scientifically tested' products have always had a prestige appeal, we do, of course, find some polysyllabic, pseudo-classical trade names, especially in the fields of hygiene and medicine:

'Anadin', 'Disprin', 'Domestos', 'Lanolin', 'Lucozade', 'Palmolive' and 'Panadol'.

The purpose of all advertising is to familiarise customers with or remind them of particular products in the hope that they will *do* something, and therefore negatives tend to be used very infrequently. When they do occur they are usually in a stressed position to emphasise the special merits of a product:

Nothing acts faster than Anadin.

Don't say 'brown'. Say 'Hovis'.

or they occur in comic sketches such as those involving the Heineken catch-phrase

Heineken refreshes the parts other beers cannot reach.

where the advertisement relies mainly on humour for its effect.

Like negatives, the past tense is usually avoided. Often, no finite verb occurs:

Daz Liquid – less pong, more ping.

Debenhams – More choice. More style. More you.

Kellogg's All-Bran – a great fibre provider.

Taste not waist. (Weightwatchers' meals)

or an imperative-type construction is used:

Get a little eXtra help from the HalifaX.

Make sure it's a Michelin.

Put a little magic into your home. (Vanish Magic Stick)

Equally common, however, is the use of verb forms which imply a universal timelessness:

Alton Towers where wonders never cease.

There's no other tea to beat P.G.

Smith's Square Crisps – They taste as good as they crunch.

On the rare occasions where the past tense is used, it stresses the long traditions associated with a product:

We've taken our whisky in many ways, but always seriously.

Sandeman Port has frequently been raised in the Members' Dining Room and, on one memorable occasion, in the House itself.

or emphasises its reliability:

We've lapped the world with tread to spare. (Dunlop Tyres)

We've solved a long-standing problem. (Pretty Polly Support Tights)

or makes an appeal to authority:

Seven out of ten children preferred these beans to the ones you probably give them.

Eight out of ten owners said their cats preferred it.

Advertising slogans resemble newspaper headlines in their tendency to use imperatives, non-past and non-finite verb forms, as can be seen if we juxtapose a number of slogans and headlines:

Fashioned by Aerospace not fashion (Saab car)	Wanted: buyer to share and share alike (*Independent on Sunday*, 8 April, 1990)
One of life's little luxuries (Imperial Leather soap)	The great rock 'n' roll rip off (*Daily Express*, 9 April, 1990)
Direct Sailings. Direct Savings (Scandinavian Seaways)	Must shop; can't stop (*Independent on Sunday*, 8 April, 1990)
Tough tools for tough jobs (Black and Decker)	Toast to the tough governor (*Daily Express*, 11 April, 1990)

Perhaps both these genres might be said to show a predilection for communicating their message in the shortest, simplest way possible, a characteristic also found in telegrams and in pidgins.

So far we have looked at some of the characteristics of the grammar of advertisements. Turning now to vocabulary we find that, like native speakers, advertisers have learnt to make 'infinite use of finite means'. Comparatively few verbs are used, the following being among the most common: 'be', 'make', 'get', 'take', 'try', 'come', 'go', 'have', 'need', 'see', 'use' and 'buy'. A similarly small set of evaluative adjectives occurs. Contemporary favourites include 'agile', 'green', 'silk', 'ozone-friendly', 'environment-friendly', 'additive-free', 'soft', 'wholesome' and 'improved'. Occasionally comparatives and superlatives occur, although since all advertisements now have to pass stringent BCAP (British Code of Advertising Practice) tests, advertisers have to be careful not to claim unprovable attributes in their products. A paint manufacturer, for example, may claim 'Advance from Crown – the paint that rewrites the rules' because it does not in fact say what the rules are or indeed why rewriting the rules should produce a more acceptable paint. But it cannot say that this product is better than Brand X. Some copywriters partly overcome this restriction by saying that no other product is better.

Kwik Fit – you can't get better.

by using 'probably':

Carlsberg – probably the finest lager in the world.

by means of a conditional clause that implies much more than it states:

If only everything in life was as reliable as a Volkswagen.

or by modifying a competitor's slogan. IBM appealed to buyers of their machines by:

I THINK THEREFORE IBM.

Amstrad capped this by displaying an IBM model costing £1,422 + VAT side by side with a similar Amstrad machine costing £749 + VAT and the words:

I THINK MORE CAREFULLY THEREFORE I AMSTRAD.

In attempting to attract attention and make slogans memorable, copy-writers frequently play on the multiple meanings of many English words. This technique is widely used in advertising alcohol:

Just drink Carleton LA and you're under the influence of nothing but yourself.

You've got to hand it to them. (Tetley's)

Royal Mail Parcel Force – the power to deliver.

but punning is prevalent in all types of advertising language. It appears, for example, in the Goldenlay Eggs campaign which advises:

Lose ounces
Save pounds.

The pun on 'pounds' is made explicit in the rest of the advertisement which promises:

You save money and stay healthy when you slim with the help of Goldenlay, natural, fresh eggs.

Nor is punning limited to commercial advertising. It has been effectively used in road campaigns such as:

Better late than the late.

and to encourage young people to think of nursing as a career. Many colour supplements carried the message

If you have the talent, we have the theatre.

Punning occurs with nouns, adjectives and verbs, sometimes singly as in:

Give your hair a touch of spring.

Hermesetas – the sweet alternative.

Don't just stick it. Bostik it.

but often in such combinations as:

Hunts (Ginger Ale). To be taken in the right spirit.

or:

There's a terrific draught in here.

which recommends a particular beer.

Punning also occurs when the meanings of similar sounding words are played on as in:

Plax helps shift plaque.

or:

Eau K. (Perrier)

One of the commonest forms of punning involves the use or modification of a well-known phrase. The value of packet tea is emphasised in:

P.G.'s worth a packet.

St. Ivel's Gold spread copy asks:

Is yours [i.e. your spread] as good as Gold?

Creditplan advertises itself as:

the Loan Arranger

and uses a cowboy logo to reinforce the link with the 'Lone Ranger'; the Leeds Building Society built a campaign on:

Say the Leeds and you're smiling [Say 'Cheese'].

and a series of television advertisements remind the viewer:

Wherever you may wander
There's no taste like Stones.

The most extended use of lexical and structural ambiguity that we could find occurred in a 1974 Pepsi Cola radio campaign where the following dialogue was used:

A   Tonight we're talking to people about Pepsi. Excuse me, you're a volcano. Is that right?

B   Either that or a large cigarette lighter.

A   Er, quite. What do you think of Pepsi?

B   Great! I drink it on the rocks. Like before I tried Pepsi I was tiny.

A   So Pepsi made a mountain out of a molehill?

B   Listen. I was so small moles used to trip over me.

A   But now you enjoy being a mountain.

B   Yeah, sure. It's a laugh a minute.

A   Incidentally, how old are you?

B   As old as the hills. (Rumbling noise) Pardon me – just a little heartburn.

C   Lipsmackinthirstquenchinacetastinmotivatingoodbuzzincool-talkinhighwalkinfastlivinnevergivincoolfizzin – PEPSI.

Like many successful advertisements, it started a fashion. It was partially imitated by milk advertisers in the mid 1980s:

Body-makin', body-buildin', body-conscious, body-language,
Anybody, everybody needs bottle.

and closely imitated by Framlington in 1990:

Lipsmackin', tax savin', Britain backin', award winnin', risk spreadin',
regular reportin', easy payin', capital buildin' PEP . . .

There are many additional aspects of the language of advertising that we could consider. It would be instructive, for example, to examine the regional deviations that occur, the use of rural accents in the promotion of dairy products, beer and bread, the type and extent of orthographic modifications, modifications that include 'kreem' for 'cream', 'Ezy Squeeze' (a juice extractor), 'Rice Krispies', 'Wisk' (automatic washing liquid) and 'Hedex' (headache tablets). Such areas of advertising language are outside the scope of a brief chapter, however, and we shall content ourselves by referring to just two further aspects of advertising language which the reader may wish to examine in greater depth.

First, there is a tendency for advertisements (and people influenced by them) to condense meaning. This is often done by means of adjectival compounds like 'country-fresh', 'farmhouse-fresh', 'lip-smackin'', 'micro-digital', 'quick-acting', 'trouble-free' and by the extensive premodification of nouns. Outside scientific journals, few nominal groups are as complex as the example given by Leech (1966):

The new four-wheel servo-assisted disc brakes

but Honda's advertisement for their range of lawnmowers states:

. . . we built a shaft drive transmission system into all our self-propelled rotary motors.

and the Toyota HR2 has:

Front and rear ventilated disc brakes

as well as a:

Tilt-adjustable steering wheel.

Such complex nominal units are, however, almost entirely restricted to written advertisements and are associated mainly with mechanical gadgetry.

Secondly, advertisements often use language in ways which are more frequently associated with poetry or oratory than with commerce. Rhyme, alliteration and syntactic parallelism are favourite devices of copy-writers and are found in the promotion of such diverse products as lawn mowers:

Why slow mow when you can Flymo?

ice-cream and confectionery:

Romanza – the extravaganza. (Wall's)

Masses of magic moments. (Quality Street)

kitchen equipment:

Installed in four days.
Guaranteed for five years. (Kitchens Direct)

newspapers:

It's a right riveting read. (*Daily Star*)

A newspaper – not a snoozepaper. (*Daily Mail*)

and political views:

Let us make this a country safe to work in; let us make this a country safe to walk in; let us make it a country safe to grow up in; let us make it a country safe to grow old in. (Mrs Thatcher)

People who can. Not people who con. (Labour)

Advertising techniques change often as a means of keeping up with an ever-changing society but also from a desire for novelty. There is nothing so dated as an out-of-date slogan! A study of the language and the imagery used by Guinness over the last sixty years, for example, shows how its advertisements were originally aimed at working-class girder-carrying men who were reminded:

Guinness is good for you.

and:

Guinness for strength.

The shape of the glass in advertisements changed from tall and straight to wine-shaped in 1973 as Guinness tried to widen its appeal to women. The mid- to late-1970s produced a series of puns:

We've poured throughout the reign.

Enjoy a phew in the shade.

Pint sighs.

The 1980s introduced the 'Guinnless' campaign where former Guinness drinkers were reminded of how good the drink could be. This campaign was not totally successful in that the copy on hoardings:

Guinnless isn't good for you.

was sometimes misread and the advertisements unintentionally created negative associations. Towards the end of the 1980s, a new campaign appealing to male and female individualists began to equate Guinness and 'Black Magic'.

When you know your own mind, it shows. Whatever you do spells individuality and style . . . It tastes as distinctive as it looks – cool, dark and sophisticated.

Although advertisers try to bring out the uniqueness of their products by the use of individualistic copy, it is also possible to see trends. Advertisements in the 1960s and 1970s often used lengthy rhymes, often sung. Rhymes are, of course, perennially attractive but the 1990 favourites are either examples of 'rime riche':

Be a smarter investor with the Alliance and Leicester.

Vosene – because we're dedicated to medicated.

or they involve using a well-known pop song, such as *Leader of the Pack*, with the words modified to laud the merits of Lurpak butter.

The family scenes also reflect the non-sexist attitudes of the time. Ariel-using men are seen ironing, Black and Decker's 'Tough tools for tough jobs' are sometimes demonstrated by women, and the money-interested man of the 1980s has been replaced in advertisements for Audi and Pearl Assurance by the caring father of the 1990s, who rushes to the birth of his second child or gets out of bed when the baby cries.

Advertising techniques change with time but they continue to make an impact on society. Because of the blend of creativity, professionalism and market research, advertising has gained the status of a minor art form, becoming, in effect, a type of literature for the twentieth-century Everyman.

The above survey suggests some of the ways in which English has been used in advertising. The language used has, to a considerable extent, been based on modifications of contemporary speech habits but much colloquial speech has also been influenced by advertising language. Sometimes a trade name has become synonymous with an object or product. Thus, 'hoover' can now refer to any vacuum cleaner and when one asks for a 'Coke' one can be served with any cola-based soft drink, including Pepsi Cola, the main competitor of Coca Cola from which 'Coke' is derived.

Advertising is found on posters, radio, television and in newspapers and cinemas. It has been criticised by Professor Richard Hoggart (1965) as a form of emotional blackmail and as an exploitation of human inadequacies. It has also been praised by many television viewers as 'the best thing on the box'. Many aspects of the language contribute to the emotive power of advertising language, the choice and order of words, the syntactic arrangement, the prestige of the speaker, the frequent appeals to authority. The British Code of Advertising Practice requires that all advertising should be legal, clean, honest and truthful but no board or committee can fully control the persuasive powers of advertising. It is a form of persuasion by which we are all affected and its full impact is to be understood in terms of both linguistic and psychological influences. Here we have attempted to show only the characteristic features of advertising language.

Additional Reading

Barnicoat, J. (1972), *Concise History of Posters* (London: Thames and Hudson).

Berman, R. (1981), *Advertising and Social Change* (Beverly Hills: Sage).

Brown, H. and Murphy, J. (1976), *Persuasion and Coercion* (Buckingham: Open University Press).

Coward, R. and Ellis, J. (1977), *Language and Materialism* (London: Routledge and Kegan Paul).

Davis, H. and Walton, P. (1983), *Language, Image, Media* (Oxford: Basil Blackwell).

Dyer, G. (1982), *Advertising as Communication* (London: Methuen).

Hoggart, R. (1965), 'Advertising – A form of emotional blackmail', *Advertisers' Weekly*, 1 October.

Key, W. B. (1976), *Media Sexploitation* (New York: Signet).

Leiss, W., Kline, S. and Jhally, S. (1986), *Social Communication in Advertising* (London: Methuen).

Mukerji, C. (1983), *From Graven Images: Patterns of Modern Materialism* (New York: Columbia University Press).

Myers, K. (1986), *Understains: The Sense and Seduction of Advertising* (London: Routledge).

Schudson, M. (1984), *Advertising: The Uneasy Persuasion* (New York: Basic Books).

Sinclair, J. (1987), *Images Incorporated: Advertising as Industry and Ideology* (London: Routledge).

Stewart, D. W. and Furse, D. H. (1989), *Effective Television Advertising* (Lexington: Lexington Books).

Watson, J. and Hill, A. (1989), *A Dictionary of Communication and Media Studies* (London: Edward Arnold).

Williamson, J. (1978), *Decoding Advertisements* (London: Marion Boyars).

Veljanovski, C. (1989), *Freedom in Broadcasting* (London: Institute of Economic Affairs).

7 English in Literature

No truly human society, it would generally be agreed, could exist without the use of a natural human language. What is perhaps less widely appreciated is that all human societies possess, in addition to a language, an artistic heritage, including a literature which embodies their history and traditions, their wisdom and beliefs.

The word 'literature' is etymologically related to 'letters' and so implies a written variety of language, but it is useful to remind ourselves that oral literature preceded and conditioned much of our written literature. The earliest English poetry which has survived is written and yet we can see in Old English poetry many linguistic devices which derive from oral verse, devices such as the regular and systematic use of alliteration, assonance, incremental repetition, the occurrence of stock phrases and, perhaps most clearly of all, the use of an attention-getting exclamation: '*Hwæt!*' Old English poetry also relied heavily on myths, traditional wisdom and on memorised family trees such as the one which traces the ancestry of the founder of Britain back to Brutus. It is also worth remembering that for many societies in the world literature is exclusively oral even today. In West Africa, for example, the history of the tribe is frequently stored in the memories of the old, the wise or the specially trained '*griot*'. Such legendary history is often related in a narrative chant which employs similar mnemonic devices to those found in Old English poetry. It would be out of place to offer a piece of African vernacular literature here, but something of the above techniques can be shown to occur in Pidgin English worksongs such as the following extempore sample recorded in Cameroon:

Masa, a wan wok o!	(Master, I want work o!)
Na wɔk dis o!	(This is work o!)
Masa, yu wan wɔk o!	(Master, you want work o!)
Na wɔk dis o!	(This is work o!)
O ya ya!	(O ya ya!)
So so dai wɔk o!	(Always killing work o!)
Mɔni no dei o!	(There is no money o!)
O ya ya!	(O ya ya!)
Mɔni no dei o!	(There is no money o!)

Wuman no dei o!	(There are no women o!)
O ya ya!	(O ya ya!)
Daso dai wɔk o!	(Only killing work o!)
Na wɔk dis o!	(This is work o!)
O ya ya!	(O ya ya!)

Oral literature is not, however, confined to remote African villages. It is part of our everyday experience in Britain and includes story-telling (true or presumed true), historical narrations, anecdotes, myths, legends, fairytales and jokes. It would not be possible in the confines of this short chapter to examine fully the linguistic and stylistic differences between oral and written literature but we can, by comparing two short sample passages, indicate the *kinds* of difference that occur.

The fairytale was originally oral but it has now become written and stylised. Let us take, therefore, the first and last sections of a written Irish fairytale and compare them with the beginning and end of a story recorded in Northern Ireland:

A   Once upon a time, long, long ago, there lived in a little house in the west of Ireland a poor widow named Macha with her son Conor.

'Mother,' said Conor one autumn evening when they were sitting at the fire together, 'we seem to be getting poorer every day. I know you give me the best part of the food and that you, yourself, must be hungry.'

From that time on Conor and his mother 'never saw a poor day' and all in the story lived happy ever after.
(Sinead De Valera, *Fairy Tales of Ireland*, New English Library, 1970, pp. 102 and 108)

B   Did you hear about what happened me in Ardboe? Well, hear dear, you nivir seen anythin' like it. There was that big of a crowd. They were shovin' and pushin' like all that, an' when I got to the edge of the crowd, divil the know I knowed where I was. It was that dark! It was pitch! An' there was a line o' buses no miss all down the road. Says I to myself, says I: 'I'll just walk past them buses till I come till our own.'

Says I to myself, says I: 'Begod an' the water'll be runnin' uproads before I go back to Ardboe.' So there you are now.

Among the differences in style and language between the written and the spoken narratives we may particularly note the following. First, there is an immediacy in B which is not found in A. This feeling of immediacy is created by the use of dialect words and phrases, by the inclusion of the addressee, 'Did you hear about what happened me?', and the phatic-like occurrences of 'hear dear', 'divil the know I knowed' and 'so there you are now'. Secondly, B makes greater use of hyperbole 'You nivir seen anythin' like it', 'It was that dark. It was pitch' and 'Begod an' the water'll be runnin' uproads'. Thirdly, A is much less spontaneous with its traditional formulaic opening 'Once upon a time' and conclusion 'lived happy ever after'. It is true that B also uses a more or less stereotyped opening and conclusion, but these are less divorced from natural, spontaneous speech. And fourthly, B makes use of such attributive devices as 'Says I' rather than the '"Mother," said Conor' technique which is characteristic of the written medium. The use of 'says' with 'I' in B is not to be equated with a dialectal usage 'I says' or 'I runs', found in various parts of Britain. It is a feature of oral narrative and used in this context by speakers who could not say *'I eats bacon and eggs for breakfast'.

We may note in addition, although it is not exemplified here, that unscripted narratives like B often begin in the past tense and switch to the non-past. In this way the story can be given an immediacy and a timelessness since it is the non-past tense which is used in English to express universal-type truths such as 'Where there's a will, there's a way'.

Although oral literature is a much livelier tradition in the English-speaking world than most people realise, it is, however, to written literature that we propose to devote most of our attention in the present chapter.

Looked at from a distance, poetry, drama and the novel are clearly distinguishable, but on closer examination, we find similarities and overlap, continua rather than discrete genres. Shakespeare's plays, for example, overlap poetry in their ability to use language 'at full stretch' (Nowottny, 1965) and at the same time they share with the novel the extended scope which allows for subtle delineation of character and careful interweaving of cause and effect. Nevertheless, different genres, because of their specific aims and traditions, have evolved individual methods of utilising language and so we shall discuss poetry, drama and the novel separately.

Although poetry is now more frequently *read* than *heard*, it is a genre which has traditionally been associated with phonic devices such as rhythm, alliteration, assonance and rhyme and so it seems sensible to consider it next to oral literature since, in many ways, it preserves and embellishes the linguistic devices found there. Poetry is, of course, a comprehensive term in that it includes such different sub-genres as epics, odes, dramatic mono-logues, elegies, lyrics and ballads. We cannot give detailed attention to any of these, but instead we shall select those linguistic features which seem to us to be in some degree characteristic of all.

Human speech may be accounted for as a succession of syllables, some of which are more strongly stressed than others. For example, the first and second syllables respectively of the English words 'lovely' and 'delightful', 'love-' and '-light-', are strongly stressed in comparison with the other syllables, '-ly', 'de-' and '-ful'. So far as rhythm is concerned, human languages fall into two distinct types according to how these two kinds of syllable are produced relative to one another. In so-called 'syllable-timed' languages, like French, all syllables are produced at equal intervals of time, with the stresses occurring at random intervals. In the other type, called 'stress-timed', it is the stresses which are produced at regular intervals, with a random number of syllables occurring between. English is a language of the second type. Thus, in Wordsworth's famous line

Earth hath not anything to show more fair

We find four stressed syllables with two unstressed syllables between the first two stresses, three between the next two and one between the last two. And in the following poem by Yeats we find four stressed syllables in each line with between eight and ten unstressed syllables.

Hurrah for revolution and more cannon-shot!
A beggar upon horseback lashes a beggar on foot.
Hurrah for revolution and cannon come again!
The beggars have changed places, but the lash goes on.
('The Great Day')

It is this occurrence of varying numbers of unstressed syllables between regular stresses which gives English poetry its characteristic rhythm, a much more organic feature than the rhyme which is popularly regarded as essential to poetry.

Although poetry derives its linguistic material from the speech of the language community, it often deviates markedly from conventional norms. The deviations which are most apparent in English poetry include the following. First, there is considerably more flexibility in the word order of poetry than of live speech. Thus, in these lines from Gray's *Elegy in a Country Churchyard*,

Some village-Hampden, that with dauntless breast
The little tyrant of his fields withstood;

we find a subject, object, verb order (SOV) whereas the usual word order in English is SVO.

Secondly, poets often transfer words from one class to another. All users of the language do this at times as, for example, when a manufacturing name like Hoover becomes a brand name and hence a verb, in 'I've just hoovered that carpet', but poets use the technique more extensively and creatively. In the following two lines from Hopkins, for example, we find two adjectives, 'terrible' and 'rude', being used as noun and verb respectively:

> But ah, but O thou terrible, why wouldst thou rude on me
> Thy wring-world right foot rock? ('Carrion Comfort')

Occasionally too we find word deletion. Often in the past, it was for the sake of rhyme or rhythm as in Herbert's:

> I will abroad ('The Collar')

but when deletion occurs in modern poetry it usually results from the compression of ideas. Thus, because Yeats chose to avoid prepositions in

> I made my song a coat

the reader may interpret the line as meaning either 'I made my song into a coat' (i.e. I protected myself by writing poetry) or 'I made a coat for my song' (i.e. I embroidered my verse) or indeed see the relevance of both interpretations.

Unusual collocations such as Keats's 'noiseless noise' or Dylan Thomas's 'a dream ago' and 'once below a time' are a regular feature of much poetry. But, just as modern poets tend to avoid the archaisms favoured in the past and found, for example, in the Keats line

> Bright star, would I were steadfast as thou art,

there seems to be a modern movement away from neologism and exoticism in vocabulary choice. Often, it is true, one finds unexpected descriptions as when Vernon Scannell refers to his wife as 'my sack of sighs' but much good modern verse seems to prefer the directness, simplicity and wit exemplified by Stephen Leslie's description of his schooldays:

> And even at the age of four
> We would drop pencils
> On the floor as she passed,
> Solely to look up her skirt
> And see God knows what.
> ('Seven Bloody Years')

Poets have also stretched the language by the exploitation of meta-phorical possibilities as in the use of images from industry by Hopkins:

> The world is charged with the grandeur of God.
> It will flame out, like shining from shook foil;
> It gathers to a greatness, like the ooze of oil
> Crushed
>
>   ('God's Grandeur')

and by the modification of traditional orthography, including punctuation. e e cummings, for example, often avoided capital letters for the pronoun 'I' and for names, including his own. He frequently took a simple expression such as 'I'm so drunk, dear' and made the reader think about its meaning by varying the expected form. Instead of a single sentence appearing on one line, the utterance is written vertically as a six-line stanza. His orthographic modifications were not haphazard, however. The slowness of speech and the unusual emphases often associated with intoxication are indicated by the spacing and the use of drunG and 'k,dear' as the two final lines.

Many younger poets studied cummings and explored the poetic possibilities offered by unconventional spacing, punctuation and grammar. Stephen Leslie's avoidance of punctuation results in the interplay of several possible meanings in 'Thoughts':

> ideas tickle the surface
>
> poke around and nose about
> think in brilliant colour
>
> let me show you the pigment of my imagination

We can read 'ideas' as the subject of some or all of the verbs 'tickle', 'poke', 'nose' and 'think'. On the other hand, 'ideas' are perhaps being instructed to 'tickle', 'poke', 'nose' and 'think'. There is a further ambiguity in the 'you'. It could be plural and refer to 'ideas' or singular and so be addressed to the reader.

Edwin Morgan, too, learned from cummings. His 'Pomander' (*From Glasgow to Saturn*, 1973, p. 155) is like an exercise in word association, where 'pomander' suggests 'poem' and 'her'; 'her' in turn triggers off the pronoun 'him'; and 'him' leads to its homonym, 'hymn'.

His space poem 'Off Course' (p. 65) is a 21-line meditation using two noun phrases per line. Each phrase is of the form 'the weightless seat' and is made up of a definite article, 'the', an adjective often associated with space and a noun.

The use of apparently discrete noun phrases with no finite verbs to indicate time is a grammatical representation of the astronaut no longer linked to earth and earth time. Morgan and other younger poets may not have repeated cummings's techniques of opening lines with a closing bracket or an exclamation mark but they saw the value of making all aspects of language and typography serve their poetic needs.

Poets often select forms which are outside the range of normal colloquial usage, but equally often they limit their linguistic choices by adhering to a restricted number of options, as for example in 'parallelism'. Sound parallelism includes alliteration, that is, consonant repetition:

> Ripens and fades and falls and hath no toil
> Fast rooted in the fruitful soil
> (Tennyson, *The Lotus Eaters*)

assonance, that is, vowel repetition as in the 'i' and 'o' sounds in the following lines from Tennyson:

> Sweet and low, sweet and low,
> Wind of the western sea,
> Low, low, breathe and blow
> Wind of the western sea!

and rhyme. The Tennyson examples illustrate complete stem rhyme, 'toil' and 'soil', 'low' and 'blow', but partial rhymes seem especially popular in modern verse and these can be seen in the 'shot' and 'foot' and 'again' and 'on' rhymes of Yeats's 'The Great Day', quoted above. Parallelism of sound does occur in natural speech. We find it in 'hear dear', 'divil the know I knowed where I was' and 'the water'll be runnin' uproads' in our oral narrative, but its occurrence tends to be sporadic and non-significant in speech whereas its occurrence in poetry is organised and controlled.

Syntactic parallelism involves the repetition of the same linguistic structure. Examples of this type of parallelism are to be found in both 'Sweet and Low' and 'The Great Day', but a more striking example can be given from Yeats's poem 'There':

> There all the barrel-hoops are knit,
> There all the serpent-tails are bit,
> There all the gyres converge in one,
> There all the planets drop in the sun.

Syntactic parallelism is also found in live speech, especially in oratory. The reader might, for example, like to look at the speeches of Martin Luther King from this point of view.

We have discussed the above linguistic features as if they occurred in isolation in poetry, but usually they co-occur and contribute to the unity and cohesion of a good poem. One of the differences between poetry and a rhymed advertisement like

> Don't spend a fortune on a trip to Mandalay
> It only costs a penny a day
> Taking the sunshine the Halibut way
> In capsule or in liquid form it's sunshine either way
> So get into the habit of just taking one a day

is that poets select words and rhymes which seem to belong together. They aim at a coalescence of form and meaning. In advertising, form is always subordinated to meaning.

The extensive use of regular patterns of sound and syntax in poetry can result in the language appearing markedly artificial:

> There passengers shall stand, and pointing say,
> (While the long fun'rals blacken all the way)
> 'Lo these were they, whose souls the Furies steeled,
> And cursed with hearts unknowing how to yield
> (Pope, *Elegy to the Memory of an Unfortunate Lady*)

and, in different ages, poets have felt the need to return to 'language such as men do speak' (Wordsworth, Preface to the *Lyrical Ballads*) but poetic language cannot and should not be identical to everyday, spontaneous speech. Occasionally, it is true, poems can *appear* to use language which closely resembles normal speech. There is often, for example, a straightforward simplicity in the language of the ballads:

> 'A bed, a bed,' Clerk Saunders said,
> 'A bed for you and me.'
> 'Nay now, nay now,' quod May Margret
> 'Until we married be.'
> (Anon., *Clerk Saunders*)

and a colloquial forcefulness in the openings of many metaphysical poems:

> For God's sake hold your tongue and let me love (Donne)

or

> I saw Eternity the other night (Vaughan)

but the similarity to live speech should not blind the reader to the precise organisation that underlies all good poetry. Indeed, it would be naive to expect poets merely to reproduce live, unpremeditated utterances. Like dramatists and novelists, poets create linguistic artefacts which will endure beyond their own time. They are stretching the language, therefore, and expanding its resources, and so, no matter how spontaneous poetic language may look or sound, it is language distilled and idealised: 'What oft was thought but ne'er so well expressed' (Pope). The apparent spontaneity of some ballads and lyrics is an illusion because the unified structure of a poem is moulded, not ready-made. Seamus Heaney, in a television discussion of his own poetry (1975), described poetic creation as 'the love act between the art and the craft', emphasising by his metaphor the need for both inspiration and labour in the writing of a poem.

Drama, like poetry, is heavily dependent on the forms and the possibilities of live speech because a play needs to use the spoken medium to achieve maximum effect.

Drama has been popular in England at least as far back as the Middle Ages, during which time many 'miracle' and 'morality' plays were written. These plays were often based on biblical themes, such as Noah and the Flood, and they were performed in or near a church with most of the community taking part, either actively by playing a role, or passively as a member of the audience. Because such drama was meant to appeal to everyone, the themes were universally interesting and the language suited all levels of society.

The tradition of producing plays which appealed to all classes and to different levels of intelligence and education was continued by the Elizabethans. Shakespeare invariably balanced his Hamlets and his grave-diggers, his Prince Hals and his enlisted men. The language of the courtly characters was usually in verse:

Hamlet: I loved Ophelia: forty thousand brothers
            Could not, with all their quantity of love,
            Make up my sum
                (Act V, Scene i)

in contrast to the prose preferred for commoners:

Gravedigger: Is she to be buried in Christian burial when
                she wilfully seeks her own salvation?

and there was occasional use of dialect forms, as in *Henry V* where Fluellen is represented as using Welsh-sounding catch-phrases like 'look you' (Act III, Scene vi) and as substituting 'p' for 'b' in:

            I'll assure you, 'a uttered as prave words at
            the pridge as you shall see in a summer's day.
                (Act III, Scene vi)

The use of non-standard English has continued to be a feature of the language of drama, often being used by modern dramatists to stress the strength and power of the working classes. Wesker, for example, approximates to the Norfolk dialect in *Roots*:

Mr Bryant:	And there she were gettin' us to solve the moral problem and now we know she didn't even do it herself. That's a rum 'un, ent it?
Mrs Bryant:	The apple don't fall far from the tree – that it don't.

(*The Wesker Trilogy*, Penguin edn, 1964, p. 144)

It should be noted, however, that Wesker's use of dialect is largely confined to pronunciation differences, detailed instructions for which are provided at the beginning of the play (p. 83), and to a number of widely occurring regional verb forms such as those used above and 'she heven't spoke' (p. 132), and to non-standard prepositional usage such as 'But I never saw the point on it' (p. 143). It is important for Wesker's purpose that his characters be shown as working-class men and women but to do this it is sufficient to *indicate* that the actors use working-class speech patterns and leave the rest to the knowledge and sensitivity of the audience.

The link between drama and religious ritual has often been commented on. Like a religious rite, a play was meant to be a communal activity. Whereas poetry and the novel normally affect the individual, drama in its transmission and its reception operates in a social context. To *read* a Shakespeare play silently and in private is to lose much of its vitality and to cause the reader to concentrate unduly on statements which go unnoticed in a performance. Problems such as 'How many children had Lady Macbeth?' arise only if one reads the play as if it were a novel or a transcript of history.

Dialogue in a play often appears more realistic than speech in either poetry or the novel because, like live speech, it is heard. Spoken dialogue is thus subject to many of the same laws as live speech. However unspontaneous such an utterance as

> To be, or not to be, that is the question,
> Whether 'tis nobler in the mind to suffer
> The slings and arrows of outrageous fortune,
> Or to take up arms against a sea of troubles,
> And by opposing, end them
> (*Hamlet*, Act II, Scene i)

might look today, it can be made to sound convincing because of an actor's use of modern rhythms, pauses and intonation patterns. The regulated rhythms of verse drama can thus be made to appear speech-like and, in literature, it is enough for dialogue to *seem* realistic. An actor can utter

Hamlet's soliloquies so that they can sound like the mental processes of a man tortured by doubt and guilt. We accept the metrically regulated and highly structured language as we accept the dramatic technique of uttering one's thoughts aloud on the stage. Both are established conventions, like the format of a poem on the page or the use of inverted commas to indicate direct speech.

Close examination of Hamlet's soliloquies also reveals that the play, as a whole, deals with themes which are universal, which investigate fundamental questions not just about a prince of Denmark but about mankind. And this point underlines a basic difference between the logical nature of the language of drama and the associative character of spontaneous utterances. Dramatists tend to use language to deal with universal 'truths' rather than with immediate facts or happenings. Historical fact suggests that Macbeth was a well-loved ruler, that Richard III was a gentle, honourable man, dedicated to justice and the divine right of kings, but such knowledge does not negate the power or psychological truth of Shakespeare's plays in which fundamental questions about power and ambition are investigated. It may well be, as Shakespeare suggested, that

> Life's but a walking shadow, a poor player
> That struts and frets his hour upon the stage
> And then is heard no more. It is a tale
> Told by an idiot, full of sound and fury
> Signifying nothing
> (*Macbeth*, Act V, Scene v)

but, if so, a play is not an accurate reflection of life. In a play we may still find the sound and the fury, but the language and the events are manipulated so that the audience is given a coherence, a logic, a significance rarely discernible in transcripts of real-life experience.

In life, speech is often an end in itself, whereas the dramatist, like the poet and the novelist, utilises language to create a particular effect and, with drama, the effect is conceived in terms of a performance. A play's interpretation may vary considerably with time – the comic Malvolio of the seventeenth century, for example, can become the sympathetic, almost tragic character of a number of twentieth-century productions – but its function as a performance, as an idealisation and stylisation of people and activities, remains relatively constant. Techniques may change. The chorus may disappear and Everyman give way to a Goldberg or a McCann. The soliloquy may become less intrusive and the dialogue may be less metrically balanced. But although modern dramatists like Pinter may utilise language which seems much closer to live speech than a Shakespearean soliloquy does, their dialogue also serves a number of integrated functions. Such phatic-like communication as

Meg:	Here's your cornflakes. Are they nice?
Petey:	Very nice.
Meg:	I thought they'd be nice. (She sits at the table). You got your paper?
Petey:	Yes.
Meg:	Is it good?
Petey:	Not bad.
Meg:	What does it say?
Petey:	Not much.

(*The Birthday Party*)

serves more than phatic function. It helps establish an atmosphere of almost stereotyped domestic boredom and gives insights into the foolish sense of expectation that is part of Meg's character and the resigned stoicism that is part of Petey's. In drama, all utterances have a relevance in terms of their moment of occurrence but also in terms of characterisation or story development. However natural an utterance may appear to be, however casual it may seem, it has, in a good play, a significance beyond its immediate occurrence.

One further similarity between live speech and its representation in drama may be indicated. Observers of both would be exposed to only the spoken medium. They would almost unconsciously make guesses as to the speaker's age and background, guesses which might be modified in the light of subsequent data. They would, for example, have to reach their own conclusions as to whether Hamlet was an idealistic youth or a man in his thirties, just as they would have to rely on their innate knowledge of society in evaluating spontaneous conversation. A member of an audience is thus in a similar position to a person who overhears and witnesses the unfolding of a story without necessarily interacting with it.

In the early modern period when documentary realism seems to have been less important to both playwright and audience than it is now, the actors were given little more than a text and a list of characters. Players performing *The Tempest*, for example, were provided with the information that Caliban was a 'deformed salvage' (i.e. savage) and they were then expected to provide their own actions, gestures and interpretations. In more recent drama, however, the actions, gestures, meaningful glances and even lighting instructions are often prescribed by the writer. In O'Casey's *Juno and the Paycock* very detailed instructions are provided with the dialogue as can be seen from the following quotations which are all taken from half a page of text:

Johnny:	(rising swiftyly pale and affected)
	(He hurriedly goes into the room on left.)

Mrs Boyle: (apologetically)

Johnny: (He rushes out again, his face pale, his lips twitching, his limbs trembling.)

Mrs Boyle: (catching him in her arms)

(*Three Plays*, Papermac edn, p. 38)

Pinter goes further than O'Casey in that he also provides stage management instructions such as the following.

> Fade to blackout.
> Fade up house. Night.
> BILL comes in from the kitchen with a tray of olives, cheese, crisps, and a transistor radio, playing Vivaldi, very quiety. He puts the tray on the table, arranges the cushions and eats a crisp. JAMES appears at the front door and rings the bell. BILL goes to the door, opens it, and JAMES comes in. In the hall he helps JAMES off with his coat.
> JAMES comes into the room, BILL follows. JAMES notices the tray with the olives, and smiles. BILL smiles. JAMES goes up to the Chinese vases and examines them. BILL pours drinks.
> In the flat the telephone rings.
> Fade up on flat. Night.
> Fade up half light on telephone box.
> A figure can be dimly seen in the telephone box. STELLA enters from the bedroom, holding the kitten. She goes to the telephone. BILL gives JAMES a glass. They drink.
> (*The Collection*, Methuen edn, pp. 32–3)

It thus appears that modern drama, which is probably read as often as it is watched, is tending to rival the novel in providing more and more background information about what a character *is* and what he *does* as well as what he says and how he says it. But drama, in spite of all the changes it has undergone, is still the most seemingly natural of all literary genres. Television may have adversely affected cinemas and theatres but it has popularised plays of all kinds, from Greek tragedy on BBC2 to soap operas on other channels.

Whereas the language of drama is necessarily related directly to speech, the language of the novel, which is probably the most popular genre of our day, is much more varied. The novel is usually read silently and in private and so it is the most closely related of all literary genres to the written medium.

There is, of course, a good deal of speech represented in novels. Indeed, as the novel has developed as a genre, speech and dialogue have come to be an essential element in it. The fictional representation of speech, however, is by no means identical with live speech.

For one thing, as we saw in Chapter 4, live speech in face-to-face situations is supplemented by paralinguistic signals which can be both subtle and complex. The novelist can include descriptive details to indicate important paralinguistic 'messages', particularly by means of such attributive verbs as 'snarled', 'thundered', 'laughed' and 'murmured', but cannot hope to reproduce the complexity of the natural speech situation in its entirety. The solution, therefore, is to supply some of the elements and leave the rest to the understanding and imagination of the reader.

Dialogue is also supported by what novelists choose to reveal in the course of the narrative concerning their characters. The readers, then, when they encounter the speech of these characters are able to infuse it with the knowledge that the writer has supplied. For example, when Graham Greene first introduces Pinkie in *Brighton Rock*, he refers to him only as 'the Boy': 'The Boy paid his threepence and went through the turnstile' (Penguin edn, p. 21). Later, this reference is supplemented with such descriptive detail as 'the slaty eyes were touched with the annihilating eternity from which he had come and to which he went', and reports of the effect he had on people: 'the stall-holder . . . eyeing him with uneasy distaste' (p. 22). In this way Greene creates for Pinkie a menacing, almost mindless ruthlessness which influences the reader's response to all the Boy's utterances, even such apparently innocuous ones as (p. 23):

'Take the doll,' the Boy said. 'It's no good to me. I just won it in one of those shooting booths. It's no use to me.'

Another area in which novelists must be content with approximation is in the representation of dialect, because of the difficulties associated with its representation. Apart from the standard language and literary Scots, no dialectal English has an acknowledged orthography. In attempting to represent dialect speech, therefore, a writer may unwittingly suggest that a character is either ignorant or comical or both. For this reason, until very recently, only Scottish writers have been willing to depict their heroes or heroines speaking dialect. Even then, the dialect was always indicated rather than accurately depicted. This point can be illustrated from the speech of Jeanie Deans in Scott's *Heart of Midlothian*. Jeanie is a dialect speaker and yet, in the following extract, we find only four clear dialectalisms.

Oh, Madam, if ever *ye ken'd* what is was to sorrow for and with a sinning and suffering creature, whose mind is *sae* tossed that she can be neither *ca'd* fit to live or die, have some compassion on our misery! – Save an honest house from dishonour and an unhappy girl, not yet eighteen years of age, from an early and dreadful death.

(Collins edn, p. 338)

And the four markings are widely known to be characteristic of Scottish dialects.

English writers have seldom felt able to take the risk of depicting a hero or heroine as a dialect speaker. As a result an author has sometimes thought it necessary to explain to the reader why certain main characters who might have been expected to speak dialect instead speak Standard English. Defoe, for example, explained that Moll Flanders had received an education far above her rank, and George Eliot claimed that Adam Bede spoke the local dialect with his mother and Standard English with others. Hardy and Lawrence also resorted to this device of implying that a major character controlled two codes: Hardy for Tess in *Tess of the D'Urbervilles* and Lawrence for Oliver Mellors in *Lady Chatterley's Lover*.

Of course, if the intention was to portray a character as ignorant and comical the use of dialect would serve very well. In *Tom Jones*, for example, when Fielding wanted to stress Squire Western's rural origins and lack of finesse, he included a few dialect features in his speech:

'Why *wout* ask, Sophy?' cries he, 'when dost know that I had rather hear thy voice than the music of the best pack of dogs in England. – Hear thee, my dear little girl! I hope I shall hear thee as long as I live; for if I was ever to lose that pleasure, I would not *gee* a brass *varden* to live a moment longer . . .'

(Penguin edn, p. 745)

But the dialect markings are not consistently maintained, as is clear from a later example of the squire's speech in which 'give' and not 'gee' is used and where 'v' is not substituted for 'f' (p. 867):

To her boy, to her, go to her. – That's it, little honeys, O that's it. Well, what is it all over? Hath she appointed the day, boy? What shall it be tomorrow or next day? It shan't be put off a minute longer than next day I am resolved . . . I thought you had been a lad of higher mettle, than to give way to a parcel of maidenish tricks. – I tell thee 'tis all flimflam.

However, the main point we wish to make concerning the use of dialect in the speech of characters in novels is that writers are conscious of the fact that it is more important for speech to *appear* realistically dialectal than for it to be an accurate transcription of the dialect speech of a particular area. It is usually sufficient to make minor adaptations of orthography, such as the use of ''ot' and ''ouse' for 'hot' and 'house', the dropping of the final 'g' in such words as 'singin'' and 'runnin'', or the use of markers such as 'ye ken' to indicate Scots and the substitution of 'v' for initial 'f' to suggest a south-western dialect, in order to give the reader the impression of dialect speech. Where dialect speech is more accurately transcribed, as it was in the original edition of *Wuthering Heights* (ch. 9):

> If Aw wur yah, maister, Aw'd just slam t'boards i' their faces all on 'em, gentle and simple! Never a day ut yah're off, but yon cat uh Linton comes sneaking hither – and Miss Nelly shoo's a fine lass! shoo sits watching for ye i' t'kitchen; and as yah're in at one door, he's aht at t'other

there are considerable dangers that the reader's understanding will be less than complete and that reading progress will be impeded.

Novelists, if they choose, can employ an idiosyncratic idiolect for narrative as well as dialogue, as Salinger does with Holden Caulfield in *The Catcher in the Rye*:

> He put my goddam paper down then and looked at me like he'd just beaten hell out of me in ping-pong or something. I don't think I'll ever forgive him for reading me that crap out loud.
>
> (Hamish Hamilton edn, p. 17)

This technique, with its use of taboo vocabulary 'goddam', 'beaten hell out of me', 'crap', and its colloquial imprecision suggested by 'or something', is excellent for implying youthful, American individuality, but such a style runs the risk of becoming tedious. It is thus usually more acceptable in small doses, in, for example, the idiolects of minor Dickensian characters. Dickens often individualises his minor characters by giving them set phrases: 'I'm 'umble', 'I'm a lone, lorn creetur', 'I shall never desert Mr Micawber', 'Peace be on this house'. Such phrases help to create an idiolectal illusion, thus enabling the reader to recognise a speaker instantly. Sometimes, too, this characterising-cum-caricaturing technique is combined with modified spellings, such as the use of 'w' for 'v' in parts of Sam Weller's speech.

So far as the narrative is concerned, it is no longer common for the author to address the reader directly, as was done in early novels such as *Tristram Shandy*, where the following direct address to the reader occurs:

> Now in order to clear up the mist which hangs upon these three pages, I must endeavour to be as clear as possible myself.
>
> Rub your hands thrice across your forheads – blow your noses – cleanse your emunctories – sneeze, my good people! God bless you –
>
> (Everyman edn, p. 461)

Nor is the reader limited to the perspectives of the author, but is more likely to be involved in the interlocking relationships between the author, the narrator and the characters. In *Wuthering Heights*, for example, the author, Emily Brontë, manipulates the reader's responses by shifting between the insights provided by two narrators, the objective, diary-keeping Lockwood and the emotionally involved Nellie Dean.

The language of the novel is not, of course, confined to speech and narrative. In most novels we find a continuum which includes thought processes and so such dichotomies as 'speech' and 'narrative', or 'direct' and 'indirect speech' really fail to comprehend the many styles of language used by a novelist. It is easy enough to decide that the following passage is direct speech and is meant to give the illusion of a live conversation:

'It is very kind of you, Mr. Knightley, to come out at this late hour to call upon us. I am afraid you must have had a shocking walk.'

'Not at all, sir. It is a beautiful moonlight night; and so mild that I must draw back from your great fire.'

(Oxford edn, p. 10)

It is equally easy to classify the following as 'narrative' (p. 15):

Mr. Weston was a native of Highbury, and born of a respectable family, which for the last two or three generations had been rising into gentility and property. He had received a good education, but on succeeding early in life to a small independence, had become indisposed for any of the more homely disputes in which his brothers were engaged; and had satisfied an active cheerful mind and social temper by entering into the militia of his county, then embodied.

Likewise one can classify this third quotation from Jane Austen's *Emma* as indirect or reported speech (p. 59):

He told me everything; his circumstances and plans, and what they all proposed doing in the event of his marriage.

But few writers limit themselves to these types. Norman Page (1973) suggests that the continuum between direct speech and narrative can be segmented into eight different speech types which he labels 'direct', 'submerged', 'indirect', 'parallel indirect', 'coloured indirect', 'free indirect', 'free direct' and 'slipping from one into another'. The segmentation of the novel's language into eight, or eighteen, overlapping categories is arbitrary, but Page's analysis does show how many and varied are the techniques employed by the novelist to involve the reader in the complexities of the plot.

Such labels as 'direct' and 'indirect' speech are therefore totally incapable of covering such novelistic representations of interior monologue as occur in the following extract from *Emma* (p. 412):

> How long had Mr. Knightley been so dear to her, as every feeling now declared him to be? When had his influence, such influence begun? – When had he succeeded to that place in her affection, which Frank Churchill had once, for a short period, occupied? –

or the representation of thought processes which are such a marked feature of the novels of James Joyce:

> I daresay the soil would be quite fat with corpse manure, bones, flesh, nails, charnelhouses. Dreadful. Turning green and pink, decomposing. Rot quick in damp earth. The lean old ones tougher. Then a kind of tallowy kind of cheese. Then begin to get black, treacle oozing out of them. Then dried up. Deadmouths. Of course the cells or whatever they are go on living. Changing about. Live for ever practically. Nothing to feed on feed on themselves.
>
> (*Ulysses*, Penguin edn, p. 110)

The novelist's portrayal of a character's thoughts clearly resembles the use of the soliloquy in drama. Both are a means of revealing the feelings and responses of a character and both are an invitation by the writer to see things from a character's point of view. Perhaps the only time in *Hamlet* that an audience sympathises with Claudius is when the king, in a soliloquy, reveals his sense of guilt and oppression.

So far we have addressed our comments primarily to the literature written by native speakers of English. Most of our comments can, of course, be applied directly to the literature written in English by people from the many parts of the world where English is not a mother tongue, but a few additional points may be helpful.

As we have seen in Chapter 3, the English language is today used in some form by approximately one billion speakers. Increasingly, it is being selected by non-mother-tongue speakers as a medium for literature. The reason for its selection is a direct result of its sheer usefulness in multilingual communities.

It is hard for people living in an essentially monolingual country to appreciate the extent of, and the linguistic difficulties associated with, the multilingualism that exists in many. The degree of multilingualism and the linguistic solution employed can differ dramatically from one country to another, but we can illustrate this range by referring to three Commonwealth countries, namely India, Jamaica and Nigeria.

India, with a population approaching 800 million, has approximately 850 languages in daily use, together with 15 official state languages (such as

Hindi and Tamil) and English in several varieties from standard to pidginised. Jamaica has under 2.5 million citizens who speak English in several forms which include Creole English, Standard British and American English and the Indianised English of the settlers from the Indian subcontinent. Nigeria has a population in excess of 96 million, as many as 400 indigenous mother tongues, three widely-used link languages, Hausa, Igbo and Yoruba, as well as English, which is again found in a range of forms from standard to pidginised.

It would not be correct to assume that the above countries represent all the linguistic possibilities found. They do, however, range from the 'monolingualism' of parts of the Caribbean to one of the most multilingual countries on earth. In addition, they comprehend a range of attitudes to the choice of medium for literary expression. All of the countries selected have rich traditions of oral literature; all have writings in English dating back several centuries; but India also has a written literature which predates the written literature of Europe, America, Africa and Australia.

The oral literature or *orature* found in most countries uses mnemonic devices such as rhythm and repetition patterns to encapsulate the distilled wisdom, customs, beliefs and culture of the group. It continues to be created and recreated in the local languages. This orature is often extremely rich. Raja Rao described the wealth of Indian oral traditions in 1937 but his points are equally valid today and apply also to Africa, the Caribbean, Asia and the Pacific:

> There is no village in India, however mean, that has not a rich sthala-purana, or legendary history of its own. Some god or godlike hero has passed by the village – Rama might have rested under this pipal-tree, Sita might have dried her clothes, after her bath, on this yellow stone . . .
> (p. 5)

In all countries too, however, contemporary creators of literature feel impelled to communicate their ideas in the written medium and for many writers the choice of language for literary expression is not clearcut. Should one write in one's mother tongue knowing that it is the language in which one can most easily express one's innermost thoughts, even if that means writing for only a few? Or should one use a world lingua franca, such as English, knowing that one will be able to address a wider audience? For some writers, such as the Nigerian Obiajunwa Wali, the choice is obvious. Writers must select their mother tongue, even if it is a minority language, and not go 'whoring after foreign gods'. For some writers too there is the knowledge that the choice of English may, in part, contribute to the death of a mother tongue, a sentiment that is expressed in 'Lament for a Dialect' by the Aborigine poet, Mary Duroux. She acknowledges that the Aborigine mother tongue, Dyirringan, is no longer the medium of the Yuin tribespeople, that the adoption of English brought about the loss not only of a language but also of a culture and that: 'To have lost you, my language, is my greatest shame.' (Gilbert, 1988, p. 28)

For other writers, the choice is not so stark. The mother tongue can and should be used for some purposes but English too must be used. For many writers brought up in the Commonwealth, English has become part of their linguistic repertoire. That does not mean that all will write in the manner of mother-tongue speakers of English. Raja Rao understood the difficulty of conveying 'in a language that is not one's own the spirit that is one's own' ([1937] 1947 edn, p. 5) and realised that Indian writers who selected the English language as their literary medium would modify it to suit their purposes:

> We cannot write like the English. We should not. We cannot write only as Indians. We have grown to look at the large world as part of us. Our method of expression therefore has to be a dialect which will some day prove to be as distinctive and colourful as the Irish or the American. (Rao, [1937] 1947, p. 5)

and Chinua Achebe expressed the views not only of Nigerians when he insisted:

> So my answer to the question, Can an African ever learn English well enough to be able to use it effectively in creative writing? is certainly yes. If on the other hand you ask: Can he ever learn to use it as a native speaker? I should say, I hope not. It is neither necessary nor desirable for him to be able to do so. The price a world language must be prepared to pay is submission to many different kinds of use. The African writer should aim to use English in a way that brings out his message best without altering the language to the extent that its value as a medium of international exchange will be lost. He should aim at fashioning out an English which is at once universal and able to carry his peculiar experience . . . it will have to be a new English, still in full communion with its ancestral home, but altered to suit its new African surroundings. (Achebe, 1965, pp. 29–30)

Writers from the Third World who opt for English as their medium of literary expression have many advantages. They are using a language with a long literary tradition, a language that has shown itself capable of describing the needs of people whether they live in the Tropics or at the Poles. It is a language capable of expressing formal and stylistic nuances and of representing a wide range of class and education. Yet, even when writers elect to write in English, they face many difficulties, the most obvious of which are naming; representing the structure of one language in terms of another; using English to represent the stylistic features of another language; and using English to represent several languages.

What should a writer call an item which has no obvious equivalent in English? Let us take an example from West Africa. In Igbo, *obanje* is the name given to a spirit that is born and reborn to a woman in a cycle of life and death. The same phenomenon is known as *abiku* in Yoruba; and most cultures in West Africa share the belief in this type of spirit child. English, however, has no equivalent. A writer could use *changeling*, but the implications are different, or use the local word and risk misunderstanding from an English-using readership. Chinua Achebe chose the latter course in his novel *Things Fall Apart* (1958) but, without full explanation of the term, many readers would miss the full terrible significance of such a description as:

> After the death of Ekwefi's second child, Okonkwo had gone to a medicine-man, who was also a diviner of the Afa Oracle, to enquire what was amiss. This man told him that the child was an *obanje*, one of those wicked children who, when they died, entered their mothers' wombs to be born again. (p. 54)

Each language is unique too in its patterning. English, for example, normally has an SVO structure where the subject precedes the verb and where the verb is followed by the object:

I saw you.

Irish, however, has a VSO structure:

Chonaic me thú. (Saw I you)

Thus even languages from the same family of languages and with a long history of contact can differ in what they say and how they say it. The differences can be much greater, however, when the languages are not closely related. When Amos Tutuola wrote *The Palm-Wine Drinkard* (1975) he recreated, probably unintentionally, many of the features of Yoruba in his English. The influence can be seen in the use of unEnglish collocations such as 'play gamble' and 'tight friends':

> . . . there was a special room in this house to play gamble . . . (p. 70)

> . . . both land and heaven were tight friends . . . (p. 118).

In Yoruba the construction *ta tete* (literally 'play gamble') means 'to gamble' and *ore timotimo* (friends tight tight) suggests 'close friends'.

When another Nigerian, Gabriel Okara, wrote *The Voice* (1970), he consciously introduced some of the SOV structures of Ijaw into his English:

'We cannot in this world ourselves recreate.' (p. 115)

Tuere still Okolo's hand gripping entered . . . (p. 126)

Often, in the hands of a good writer, this technique produces a poetic effect. The meaning is clear but the structures help the reader to realise that a culture other than an English one is being evoked.

Writers from parts of the world where English is only one of a repertoire of languages frequently have to represent a variety of languages through English. This may be done by employing linguistic and stylistic modifications to recreate a non-English culture (a culture where the local religion and the dramatic and musical traditions, for example, do not readily translate into English). The varieties may be close to international norms or they may be part of a continuum from standard English to the English-based pidgins and creoles which are found along the trade routes of the world.

Caribbean writers were among the earliest to cultivate a regional variety for literary purposes. Louise Bennett manipulates the entire spectrum of English in Jamaica for poetic effect. She uses the creole, not just for humour but for satire and political comment. The creole, as the language of the poor and uneducated, often has a sharpness and vitality that the standard language can lack:

> *Me glad fi see yuh come back, bwoy,*
> *But lawd, yuh let me dung;*
> *Me shame a yuh so till all a*
> *Me proudness drop a grung.*
>   ('The Little Twang', Morris, 1983)

(I'm glad to see you've come back, boy,/ but Lord, you've let me down;/ I'm so ashamed of you that/ my pride has dropped to the ground.)

West African writers too have exploited the range of Englishes in their country. In Chinua Achebe's early novels, Nigerian Pidgin was used tentatively, mainly for humour, but both he and other writers came to see that it was a linguistic seam that could be profitably mined. Segun Oyekunle wrote what he described as 'the first play to be published entirely in pidgin' (i.e. Nigerian Pidgin) in 1983. In *Katakata for Sofahead* (Confusion for Sufferhead), Pidgin becomes a language of truth, the lingua franca of prisoners who comment, not just on their own condition, but on the corruption that is part of modern society:

Bot you sabi how dem dey get de money? Make we talk true talk, I nefer see dat person for dis dontry we dey get im money wit bitter sweat wey go dey spray am yafu-yafu like so for public . . . (pp. 13–14)

(But you know how they get the money? Let's talk the simple truth, I have never seen a person in this country who got his money through hard toil who spends it lavishly in public . . .)

Frank Aig-Imoukhuede (1982) found Pidgin a suitable medium for grief and for political comment, and more recently still in *Sozaboy* [Soldierboy]: *A Novel in Rotten English*, Ken Saro-Wiwa welds English both standard and non-standard and Pidgin to create a Nigeriaspeak that prevents a fast, superficial reading:

As we were waiting now, Bullet called me.
'Sozaboy,' he said.
'Yes, Oga.' [Boss]
'Something must happen today, Sozaboy.'
'Whasmatter?' is what I asked.
'E dey me for body like something go happen,' he replied. 'And when that thing happen, I want you to help me. I think you understand?' So I told him that I have understand. That I will help him whether whether because I like him and he is even like my brother. (p. 106)

Nissim Ezekiel (1976), the Indian poet, also uses a range of Englishes, including an English which reflects many of the uses of middle-class Indians. His awareness of the differences between such English and the international standard is clear from the titles of such poems as 'Very Indian Poem in Indian English'. In a few words, he can create a linguistic setting that is undeniably Indian. In 'Goodbye Party for Miss Pushpa T.S.', he introduces us to a character, 'You are all knowing . . . what sweetness is in Miss Pushpa . . .'. She is from 'very high family' and smiles 'simply because she is feeling'.

In spite of, or perhaps because of, the humour associated with this specifically Indian English, Ezekiel can use the medium to comment on the problems faced daily by many Indians, such as the railway clerk to whom 'no one is giving bribe' even though he is 'never neglecting [his] responsibility'. His recreation of Indian English is based on five features: the non-use of an article before 'very high' and 'bribe'; the non-occurrence of 'there' in 'what sweetness [there] is in Miss Pushpa'; the use of 'feeling' without a complement; the use of the progressive with verbs such as 'know' and 'neglect'; and the use of the singular as in 'responsibility' where most speakers of international English would use a plural.

Many of the above techniques have been used by writers whose mother tongue is not Standard English and they have helped to forge a set of voices that can be understood by all speakers of English but which could not be confused with an English or an American voice.

Literature is art, but the literary artist is fundamentally different from other artists in that the medium is already structured and meaningful. It derives its meaning from its everyday use by the language community in an infinite variety of situations to which it is able to respond by an infinite flexibility of form. The writer, as artist, does not detach the medium from its everyday use, but instead maintains contact with it in order to adapt and organise the meanings generated there with the aim of 'holding a mirror up to nature' (*Hamlet*). For this reason, literature is the most complex of the arts, but at the same time the most precise and the most accessible to all of us.

Additional Reading

Achebe, C. (1958), *Things Fall Apart* (London: Heinemann).

—— (1965), 'English and the African writer', *Transition*, 18.

—— (1972), *Girls at War and Other Stories* (London: Heinemann).

Aig-Imoukhuede, F. (1982), *Pidgin Stew and Sufferhead* (Ibadan: Heinemann Educational Books).

Amadi, E. (1972), *The Concubine* (London: Heinemann).

Ashcroft, B., Griffiths, G. and Tiffin, H. (1989), *The Empire Writes Back* (London: Routledge).

Carter, R. and Nash, W. (1989), *Discourse Stylistics* (Oxford: Blackwell).

Cluysenaar, A. (1976), *Introduction to Literary Stylistics* (London: Batsford).

Corns, T. (1989), *Milton's Language* (Oxford: Blackwell).

cummings, e e (1964), *Poems 1923–1954* (New York: Harcourt, Brace & World, Inc.).

Ezekiel, N. (1976), *Hymns in Darkness* (Delhi: Oxford University Press).

Fowler, R. (1977), *Linguistics and the Novel* (London: Methuen).

Freund, E. (1987), *Return of the Reader: Reader-Response Criticism* (London: Routledge).

Gilbert, K. (ed.) (1988), *Inside Black Australia* (Penguin Books Australia).

Johnson, C. (1988), *Dalwurra* (University of Western Australia).

Leech, G. N. (1969), *A Linguistic Guide to English Poetry* (London: Longmans).

Leith, D. and Myerson, G. (1989), *The Power of Address* (London: Routledge).

Lim, C. (1987), *Or Else, the Lightning God and Other Stories* (Singapore: Heinemann).

Macpherson, P. (1989), *Reflecting on Jane Eyre* (London: Routledge).

Morgan, E. (1973), *From Glasgow to Saturn* (Cheadle, Cheshire: Carcanet Press).

Morris, M. (ed.) (1983), *Selected Poems: Louise Bennett* (Kingston, Jamaica: Sangster's Book Stores).

Nash, W. (1989), *Rhetoric: the Wit of Persuasion* (Oxford: Blackwell).

Newton, K. M. (1990), *Interpreting the Text: A Critical Introduction to the Theory and Practice of Literary Interpretation* (London: Harvester).

Nowottny, W. (1965), *The Language Poets Use* (London: Athlone).

Okara, G. (1970), *The Voice* (London: Heinemann).

Oyekunle, S. (1983), *Katakata for Sofahead* (London: Macmillan).

Page, N. (1973), *Speech in the English Novel* (London: Longman).

Penrith, M. (1980), *Sub-styles in Emma*, unpublished M.Litt. thesis, University of Lancaster.

Rao, R. ([1937] n.d.), *Kanthapura* (New Delhi: Orient Paperbacks).

Saro-Wiwa, K. (1985), *Sozaboy: A Novel in Rotten English* (Port Harcourt: Saros International Publishers).

Selvon, S. (1971), *A Brighter Sun* (London: Longman).

Soyinka, W. (1967), *Idanre and Other Poems* (London: Methuen).

Spencer, J. (1965), 'A note on the "steady monologuy of the interiors" ', *Review of English Literature*, vol. 6, no. 2, pp. 35–41.

Tutuola, A. (1975), *The Palm-Wine Drinkard* (London: Faber and Faber).

8 English in the Classroom

Language is the most characteristically human of all our activities. It enters naturally, and essentially, into virtually everything we do, from greeting an acquaintance to making a trip to the moon. And most of the time we pay no more attention to it than we do to breathing or walking.

If we think about it at all it is probably in the simplest of terms. We see it as a means of communication, a mere bearer of messages from one person to another. Sometimes, it is true, the message itself is recognised as complex – if it is a Shakespeare sonnet, let us say, or a lecture on nuclear physics – but the complexity of the message is not seen as affecting the means by which it is transported and so, even in such cases, the function of language is considered to be essentially simple.

But such a view seriously underestimates the intimate part played by language in so much of what we do and are. Even were it true that language is simply a means of communication, it would still be impossible to separate the content of a message from the form, for the only real existence a message has is in the language which embodies it. Language does not *carry* messages, that is to say, it *creates* them. Besides, language is much more than a means of communication. That intimacy we discern between message and medium exists also in the relationship between language and thinking, perceiving, believing, working, playing and, not least, learning.

It is this centrality of language to learning that is recognised in the Kingman Report claim that:

> In the school curriculum English is unique: the child begins to acquire language before school; without it no other processes of thought and study can take place. (DES, 1988a, 1.4)

There are a number of alternative theories about what the learning process involves, though nobody can really claim to be certain. But in very general terms it would seem to involve each of us in constructing our own personal cognitive map of reality, by applying innate, probably species-specific, intellectual mechanisms to sense data, which for human beings critically include data in language form. Given normal circumstances, young children will learn not only how to make use of this crucial data in building up their own picture of the universe, but also how to stimulate and control the data by their own activity.

The internal representation thus arrived at is not simply some kind of intellectual network. There are other very important dimensions. Thus, the Kingman Report recognises that

> English teachers are inevitably concerned with pupils' intellectual, social, personal and aesthetic development. We therefore consider these four aspects of children's growth and comment on the importance of language to each — bearing in mind that each must be considered in relation to the others. (DES, 1988a, 2.9)

As has been suggested, the acquisition process begins before the child comes to school. Ideally, pre-school children have the close and exclusive attention of another person more or less whenever they demand it. One adult, usually the mother, will participate regularly in all activities, and there will be a varying number of others who respond from time to time. And in all this interaction with others, language will be used to instruct, forbid, scold, invite, entertain, ask and answer; both by the children and by the others. Their development is, thus, fused with language activity, which no more has an existence separate from that development than do all the other activities of walking, crawling, feeling, touching, tasting, seeing and hearing.

But the function of language in the learning process is even more complex and intimate than that, for the efficient assimilation of new data to an existing intellectual structure demands that many incoming sense data be reformulated in language terms for presentation to the learning mechanisms. More simply, the growth of understanding depends upon the ability to reflect on new data in relation to previous knowledge, in order to construct a comprehensive picture of reality which incorporates both old and new. Language provides the means by which such reflection may be most efficiently accomplished.

Reflection may be internal or external. Concerning the former, verbal thought, we shall have nothing to say, beyond remarking that it is presumably a characteristically human kind of thought, which would be impossible if language were not already acquired. Use of language for external reflection involves either spoken discussion in which ideas are reasoned out and clarified for oneself and others, or written composition, the importance of which was remarked upon in Chapter 1. Writing is clearly not, however, part of the normal pre-school situation.

The classroom situation contrasts with the 'natural' process. Most obviously, control of the child's incoming language data, and most other data, is exercised by the teacher. The teacher provides information and the pupil absorbs it. No doubt new and important information is made available to the child in this way, and the effective teacher will always know how to engage the interest of pupils and stimulate their desire to learn. But if questions are asked they tend to be the teacher's: if the pupils have questions they will usually go unanswered. What is worse, they may remain unasked. As for the teacher's questions, they will be unhelpful if they challenge the memory rather than the understanding – by demanding information rather than reasoning – and in this way, foster a belief that learning is all about remembering what the teacher tells you.

It could be argued that most of the limitations of the classroom situation are inherent and so unavoidable. On one side is an adult, the teacher, and on the other a relatively large number of children or adolescents. The pressure this disparity of numbers imposes on a teacher can only properly be appreciated by someone who has actually taught, but if total chaos is to be avoided a considerable degree of control must be exercised, by the teacher, over who is allowed to speak, when and to whom. And to make such control possible a framework of expectations has to be created within the classroom, in which teacher and pupil are assigned well-defined roles.

It is not being suggested that teachers are consciously aware of imposing such a framework. What happens is that young children come to school for the first time, with their own set of expectations, acquired from years of successful learning, and find that they have to come to terms with an entirely novel learning situation which is at odds with their previous experience in important respects. In such circumstances teachers may well feel that they will make things easier for everyone if they do most of the talking themselves, assigning occasional opportunities to individual pupils in order to monitor how well what they themselves are saying is being understood and remembered. And to simplify matters further they control the type of utterance the pupil may produce by sticking to straightforward information-type questions. In this way the classroom situation is likely not only to redefine the place of language in the learning process, but also what we mean by 'learning' itself.

Things might be different. The classroom situation does impose some new expectations, but there is no real reason, apart from the convenience of the teacher, why questions should be limited to information-type or the children discouraged from asking questions of their own. The role the children are asked to acquire should be one which fosters a preference for reason and understanding rather than raw dogma. To this end the teacher should learn to ask more 'why' questions and fewer 'what' questions, and should train the children by instruction and personal example to formulate questions which are precise and relevant.

Certainly, there is nothing inherent in the classroom situation which enforces ineffectiveness in the teaching of writing. In practice formal teaching of this important skill is confined to the early stages of its acquisition. What usually happens after that is that the child is not so much taught as tested, by being regularly required to produce a piece of writing for the teacher to inspect in order to detect mistakes of spelling or grammar.

Revealingly, teachers commonly refer to writing so produced as a 'pile of correction'. But since this rather negative process appears to achieve little by way of improvement, a growing number of teachers have given it up altogether. They continue to encourage the production of pieces of writing, but as acts of self-expression, which can be praised in terms of qualities such as 'sincerity' or 'spontaneity', but rarely corrected or evaluated. The alternative to negative teaching is, for some, no teaching at all.

The basic weakness here lies in the training system, which can fail to prepare teachers to give instruction in reading and writing beyond the elementary stages. This is a result of the common misapprehension that language is only a medium of communication, so that once the bare mechanics of reading and writing have been acquired all that is necessary is practice. Even so, many teachers could do a lot more than they do to explore ways of introducing positive instruction into 'composition' classes, and, at least in the secondary school, to encourage the use of writing as a reasoning and reflexive medium.

The problems created by the classroom situation are essentially the same for all children. But some children seem to arrive at school better equipped to tackle these problems than others. Partly, no doubt, it is a matter of intrinsic intellectual and personality differences, but partly too it is attributable to differences of pre-school background. Children who have had the attention of sensitive and interested adults who have taken an active part in stimulating and encouraging them to learn, for example, are more likely to respond positively to the expectations of the adult in the classroom than those who have never had the benefit of such attention. Likewise, children who have become accustomed to books as a source of knowledge and pleasure, through being read to regularly, will feel more at home in the classroom world of books, of reading and writing, then those whose pre-school preparation for literacy has been limited to occasional glimpses of the tabloid press.

Such differences are a matter of attitude, or of motive. There may also be differences of skill in the actual use of language. There is, for example, the important matter of style. As we saw in an earlier chapter, the ability to adapt one's style to the demands of different language situations is a crucial element in the effective use of language. It is as important in the classroom as it is elsewhere. During the school day, subjects change, teachers change, levels of formality change, aims change; and each change demands its stylistic response. But the range of style young children bring to school depends entirely upon what they have had an opportunity to practise in the society in which they have spent their pre-school years, and some societies offer more opportunity, and over a wider range, than do others. Some children, therefore, are bound to arrive at school lacking the necessary skill to respond to the varying stylistic demands of the classroom. It is not simply a matter of failure to acquire particular styles: as we saw earlier, style is a continuum rather than a set of discrete possibilities. The problem is the more profound one of failure to develop the essential flexibility. Children handicapped in this respect may be alienated from teacher and school at the very start. At the least, they are likely to appear backward, possibly even linguistically defective, to an insensitive teacher, and the impression created may affect the teacher's expectations of or attitudes towards such children. And early impressions can follow children right through their school career.

Moreover, it should be noted that children whose pre-school language experience has excluded the necessity to make their meanings linguistically explicit may well find it very difficult to accept the requirements of the written medium, where skill in making use of the lexical and syntactic resources of the language to achieve such explicitness is essential. Considering the extreme importance which attaches in the educational context to the need to be able to write effectively, this difficulty could prove particularly damaging.

The difficulties we have been considering involve differences in the ability to use language, and are in essence distinct from the question of which socio-regional variety the child speaks. The latter, however, cannot be ignored as a possible source of difficulty. Most children arrive at school to discover that their own language is not quite that of the teacher and the classroom, perhaps indeed that it is markedly different. The teacher will usually speak Standard English, the child some non-standard socio-regional English, or possibly even a creole. Children who have been brought up in literate surroundings, where there is familiarity with books and where the speech of the home corresponds to the language of those books, will at least have the advantage on coming to school of speaking and understanding the language of reading and writing. The others may find themselves having to acquire a new language system at the same time as they are struggling to adapt to the new learning situation.

What has just been said is not intended to contradict the now generally held opinion, following research in the United States, that one variety is as good as another at expressing complex ideas logically. But the truth is that in English-speaking communities success in education, and in most other spheres, depends heavily upon the ability to speak, read and, above all, write, Standard English. Since, as we saw in Chapter 1, reading and writing are taught, at least initially, by way of spoken language, it follows that children whose spoken vocabulary and grammar correspond to the written language from the start have a practical advantage over those whose vocabulary and grammar deviate. To recognise this truth is not to be an elitist but a realist.

Fortunately, the modern attitude to socio-regional linguistic variety is a great deal more enlightened than was the case even a short time ago, and dialect English is no longer seen simply as incorrect English, to be rooted out at all costs. The prevailing view in pedagogic circles is the one adopted by the Kingman Report:

. . . The dialect usages of family and immediate circle are sufficient to their purposes; but membership of the smaller group entails membership of the larger, and for the wider community — that of the nation and the world — the standard language will be indispensable. Of course, in acquiring the standard language, we do not abandon the variation — each has its own authenticity, and to move with facility between them is to develop a versatility in language, a linguistic repertoire, which should be open to all. (DES, 1988a, 2.5)

In fact, experience has shown that dialect speakers readily acquire the standard language for both writing and speech. The history of Standard English, which we briefly sketched in Chapter 2, demonstrates just that.

But what about the child who comes to school for the first time speaking a language other than English? In some areas of the country this has become a common occurrence. What are the long-term prospects for such children in an English-speaking education system? Clearly, there are bound to be problems initially: learning a completely new language would appear to be more difficult than acquiring variations on an existing one. However, though there is a real obstacle here, and perhaps a serious one, it can be overcome, and with informed help non-English-speaking children can acquire full control over Standard English in speech and writing. This has long been the experience, after all, of large numbers of African children, who arrive at school for the first time speaking only a local African language, but who nevertheless are able to reach the highest academic levels using Standard English or French. Indeed, in some parts of Africa, notably Cameroon, many who began life in remote villages now function at the top in government, industry and commerce, in both these languages.

Naturally, children whose mother-tongue is not English should never under any circumstances be made to feel that the language of the home is somehow inferior to English. Like dialect-speaking children they are not being asked to replace their first language by another, but rather to add a new language for reasons of its utility. They may, therefore, continue to use at home the language they have always used there.

However, there have recently been calls for non-English-speaking children to be educated through the medium of their first language rather than through English. One can fully understand the good intentions underlying such views. After all, the Unesco report on *The Use of Vernacular Languages in Education* (Paris, 1953) insists that a child's mother tongue is the most suitable medium for education. Nevertheless, even if it were practicable to teach through the medium of the 100+ languages in use in Britain, the classroom segregation implicit in such a practice would almost certainly have negative consequences. Eventually all children will be obliged to work in an environment where English is not only the language of the inhabitants of Britain, but also the preferred link language of hundreds of millions of people around the world. The personal consequences of a failure to acquire full mastery of spoken and written English in the classroom would be very serious. The consequences to society are incalculable.

Within the limitations imposed by the classroom situation on the one hand and the child's knowledge and ability on the other, the teacher teaches and the pupil learns. Evidently this latter process is the primary one, and in two senses. First, it is the justification for the entire educational system, which is designed to foster and control it. And secondly, it would appear at least desirable to understand how learning takes place before deciding how teaching is to be carried out. Unfortunately, it has to be admitted with regard to this second point that what is desirable has not so far proved attainable and that reliable knowledge is very hard to come by, with the result that teaching practices commonly owe more to accumulated experience than to the results of research. Possibly that is what educationists mean when they claim that teaching is not a science but an art.

Nevertheless, though the details of the learning process remain obscure, it is not true that we know nothing at all. It is clear, for example, that it is an active process and not a passive one; that it is not simply a matter of remembering. Accordingly, it does not so much involve the transmission of knowledge from one person to another as the construction by each individual of a reliable internal representation of the external universe, by reference to which we are able to behave intelligently towards that universe. The teacher's part in the process is to make available the raw material, to focus attention, and to encourage and facilitate the work of construction by intelligent use of questions, prompts, examples, explanations, reasons, exhortation and praise; but the pupil has to do the actual building.

It is well understood, too, that the intellectual mechanisms implicated in learning evolve through a series of stages of development associated with maturational processes. It follows from this that for much of their school career children's internal representation of the universe differs in some respects from that of their teacher, and that in an important sense they inhabit different worlds. The teacher must be aware of the difference, and of its consequences, one of which will be, since meaning for each of us must be defined in terms of our own picture of the world, that the child may *mean* something different from the teacher by one and the same utterance. The child's apparent ability to use 'because' correctly, for example, is not necessarily reliable evidence that pupil and teacher share an understanding of the relationship of cause and effect.

Teachers should also be aware of the crucial part played by language in learning, at every stage of intellectual development. Language does not itself bring the learning mechanisms into existence, of course, that being a matter entirely of maturation, but it is the most effective means by which we may take advantage of them, because, whatever the subject, language is an essential element in what has to be learned; it is impossible to separate the one from the other. Besides, in what we have called its reflexive function language gives us access to what we already know in a form which makes it possible to relate to it what we are trying to learn. The effort to reconcile the old with the new in one coherent account increases our understanding of both, reveals the gaps in our knowledge and makes possible the internal systematisation of what otherwise would remain vague private intuitions.

Since a course in psychology is universally recognised as an essential part of teachers' professional training, it is probable that they will know at least something of what there is to be known about the learning process as it relates to their pupils. They are unlikely, on the other hand, to know very much about the part language plays in this process. Indeed, they would be exceptional if they knew anything much about language, for the assumption implicit in training courses generally is that formal study either of language in general or the language one speaks in particular is unnecessary. Courses in 'English', consequently, are often concerned exclusively with literature; and not always English literature. It is also currently fashionable, it is true, to offer trainee teachers courses in 'Communication' or 'Media Studies'. Doubtless such courses offer valuable benefits, but they do not necessarily illuminate the nature and function of language in a practical way.

In order to make sensible judgements about what to encourage and what to reject, teachers need to understand, among other things, the real nature of dialect and its relationship to the standard language. They should be aware, for example, that the choice of Standard English as the medium of instruction is not a consequence of its having any intrinsic superiority. They must, on the other hand, acknowledge that there is such a thing as extrinsic superiority, that the English-speaking world attaches high prestige to Standard English in a great many contexts, and particularly the more formal ones. And so, though they ought to be tolerant of the occasional use of dialect English in contexts where they judge it may help their pupils, for example, in informal discussion, teachers must not be seduced by social or linguistic egalitarian arguments into the belief that Standard English does not matter. It does.

So far as accent is concerned, teachers have to realise that this phenomenon has arisen as a consequence of the process of standardisation through the written medium, and that the notion of 'standard' does not imply any particular pronunciation of English.

Teachers must also understand the nature of style. They must, first of all, adopt a realistic attitude towards 'correctness', and see it, not as an absolute quality, but as a relative one, dependent upon criteria of appropriateness. They must recognise that codification of English, or any language, for the purpose of reducing it to a set of written rules of grammar involves a process of idealisation which, of necessity, refines out a great deal that is essential to language in actual use. And secondly, they must be able to distinguish a lack of stylistic flexibility from grammatical or lexical deficiency. The recommendation of the Kingman Report concerning teaching aspiring teachers *about* language are, accordingly, very welcome.

Lacking the guidance of real knowledge, teachers often come to rely on folk-wisdom, on the popular myths and legends about language. Dialect, for example, may be thought to have desirable properties, such as vigour and honesty, which 'proper' English lacks, and yet at the same time be thought in some ill-defined way undesirable. Particular accents will be praised as 'nice', or, alternatively, condemned as 'ugly' or 'slovenly': value judgements which all too easily come to embrace the unfortunate human beings themselves whose speech manifests the accent in question. The grammar book and the dictionary are both accorded the status of law and given absolute priority over appropriateness, and even effectiveness, so that pupils are often instructed, for example, to 'speak in sentences', whatever the circumstances. It is essential that pupils' difficulties be diagnosed accurately so that appropriate help may be offered, and for this reason it is important that they be encouraged to speak, and to reason out difficult points aloud. Insistence upon grammatical absolutes, however, discourages any kind of exploration in speech, and ensures that nothing will be said which gives any kind of clue to pupils' problems, or even suggests that there are any.

The adverse effects of inaccurate knowledge and belief about language do not stop at unhelpful judgements concerning the pupils' English. Linguistically ill-informed teachers are unlikely to be insightful concerning their own language behaviour.

Too many teachers, for example, use their address system as a weapon. Thus, the girl who is usually called 'Mary' suddenly finds herself 'Miss Smith', and accepts the change as a sign of mild disapproval. That is legitimate. Teachers, like other users of the language, must vary their style in response to changes they perceive in the situation, and if Mary is in need of a gentle rebuke, then addressing her as 'Miss Smith' may well produce the desired response. What is not legitimate, however, is to address different members of the same class differently: some by first name, some by last, for example, or to use pejorative address terms such as 'dozy' or 'dopey', either to groups or to individuals. Charitably, one supposes this kind of language is used in ignorance. Any teacher who understood the devastating effect such behaviour can have on the individual would surely eschew it completely.

Some errors are more subtle. The teacher's manner, facial expression, posture, tone of voice, may all convey respect or disrespect, affection or dislike, either for people or for ideas, more effectively than words; perhaps even in contradiction to actual words. Feelings of aversion for particular pupils, their religious beliefs, their work, their dress, their language, possibly even their race, sex or colour, may be unwittingly communicated to them in these paralinguistic ways, while the teacher, conscious that he ought not to entertain such feelings, and knowing certainly that he should never give expression to them, is striving to maintain a strict professional neutrality in what he actually says. The pupils, for their part, may have their attitudes subtly shaped by paralinguistic persuasion which is more effective, perhaps, for being unsuspected.

Teachers, therefore, must know and understand about language if they are to be able to use it sensitively and constructively. Knowledge and understanding are if anything even more necessary in teaching it.

It is a commonplace that in an English-speaking society every teacher is a teacher of English. It might be more accurate to say that whatever teachers believe themselves to be teaching on any given occasion they will also, knowingly or not, be teaching English: for two reasons. First, languages are not acquired for their own sakes, as abstract formal systems separated from content, but as part of the process of their use in real situations for real purposes. Only actual performance is real; and the speaker/hearer's internalised grammar, like the linguist's idealisations, depends entirely upon it. Secondly, the other side of the same coin, the content of a subject cannot be separated from the ability to talk and write about it. Subjects such as physics and chemistry might seem to offer exceptions to this generalisation, since natural human languages have proved inadequate for their more advanced concepts and highly specialised ways of talking and writing about them have had to be developed. But the point about this is that without an adequate language these concepts could never have been formulated, could not be discussed, could not be communicated or taught. It remains true, therefore, that language is an essential part of the approach to every subject, not merely the means by which information about it is transmitted from person to person.

Attempting to teach a subject without taking adequate account of the language dimension by guiding and instructing pupils how to talk and write about it coherently and clearly is likely to end in vague perceptions rather than useful knowledge: the 'I know what I want to say but can't find the words' syndrome. Attempts to teach the language of a subject without taking account of its content, on the other hand, end in verbalism, with the pupils using terminology of whose meaning they have only the slightest grasp. One has encountered, for example, the literature student whose fondness for terms such as 'diction', 'imagery', 'deconstruction', 'subtext' or 'polarities' is mere imitation of an admired teacher and often masks ignorance of the phenomena named. Mimicry and rote learning, therefore, are not enough.

In practice, few subject-teachers will accept any responsibility for the language of their pupils. Even in their own specialist area they will prefer to attribute language shortcomings to failure on the part either of the primary teacher or the teacher of English. Such a view reflects the common belief that languages are acquired through instruction alone, after which they become available for use. As we have seen, form and content are essentially inseparable and use is, accordingly, itself part of the acquisition process.

Nevertheless, it is true that some instruction is also necessary, and that is formally recognised as the responsibility of the primary teacher and the teacher of English.

Their principal responsibility is of course concerned with the inculcation of literacy. For many pupils this also means being taught a variety of the language they have never used before, Standard English, and being encouraged and guided in the use of this variety in speech as well as writing; though not to the exclusion of their own dialect. Because of the influence of television and radio, this new variety will not be entirely unfamiliar to most children and learning to use it may be less unnatural than it was in former times, but it remains true that the majority of people acquire it through and for use in the written medium, and for very many it never becomes the normal variety for speech. On the other hand, many children who come to school speaking a non-standard variety of English evidently do learn to read and write in the standard dialect fairly readily, and some eventually adopt it as their normal dialect in speech.

Reading, as we saw in Chapter 1, is not merely a matter of being able to produce appropriate noises in response to marks on paper. For many people, however, including teachers, this represents a level of attainment at which instruction may stop, to be replaced by encouragement and the opportunity to practise. Two very helpful developments in the last 25 years, have been the increasing provision of school libraries and the growth of interest in children's literature (of all kinds). To make the best use of such facilities, pupils have to be taught, when necessary, how to relate text to accompanying diagram or illustration, how to use an index properly, how to search out the works which contain the information they want through the use of the library index and other sources. In seeking knowledge, they must be taught how to read actively, rather than passively, by questioning the text, reflecting on it, re-reading it, evaluating it, comparing and relating it to previous knowledge. And in seeking pleasure from books they must learn that responding to literature is more than a matter merely of being able to follow the story, that an active approach here too brings an increase of reward. Reading purposes, however, vary and do not always demand the same degree of application; nor does all reading material merit equal attention. Pupils, therefore, need to be taught to vary their reading strategy according to the ends for which they are reading, and the quality of the material. They must be ready to skim as well as ponder. In short, pupils must be taught to apply their intelligence in reading and not simply how to turn what has been written down into speech.

Writing is complementary to reading; and just as the ability to say aloud what has been written down represents the very lowest level of attainment in reading skill, so there is a good deal more to writing than being able to represent on paper what has been said. Certainly the elementary motor-skill which makes it possible to do this must be taught, but that is where learning to write begins, not where it ends.

Writing calls for the ability to construct grammatical sentences and coherent paragraphs. Admittedly, sentences do occur in speech, particularly in more formal styles, but the sentence unit is not a condition of spoken utterance in the same way that it is of writing. As for the paragraph, as the '-graph' suggests, this is a unit only of written language. Skill in the construction of both these units, therefore, is properly taught as part of the teaching of writing.

What is necessary is demonstration followed by much practice, preferably in relation to real writing needs, such as, for example, making geography or history notes. With the sentence, the pupil can be shown simple patterns to copy and then imitate; then more complex patterns once the simple ones have been mastered. If this is done systematically pupils not only develop control over a large number of sentence patterns, but learn how to modify them in order to create new acceptable patterns of their own. The paragraph is taught by taking pupils carefully through the stages of construction: showing them how to collect and select relevant information, put it in the most effective order, construct an introductory sentence and set the information down using a variety of sentence patterns to avoid monotony.

But the formal skills of sentence and paragraph construction are only part of the story. Style, the ability to write differently in response to different situations, also has to be taught and practised. This is where the co-operation of subject-teachers can be very helpful. They all require written work from their pupils. They should be encouraged to identify and analyse such requirements and to provide examples, so that teachers of English can give appropriate instruction and guidance. And teachers of English themselves have a variety of writing needs to exploit: creative, reflexive, descriptive. But the needs they exploit should be real. Pupils grow up to inherit a real linguistic world. They cannot adequately be prepared for it by artificial linguistic means.

Clearly it cannot all be done at once, and in any case instruction must be appropriate to the stage of linguistic development of the pupil. Grading is therefore essential. At the earliest stages of the primary school, for example, say up to about age 8 for most children, there is relatively little syntactic complexity and the teacher cannot expect anything more than simple sentences about everyday activity. From about age 7, the brightest children begin to be capable of more complex construction, but are still unable to displace themselves in time or space, or imagine themselves in someone else's shoes. The ability to do this comes at about age 9, though thinking is still more or less tied to the concrete until about age 15, after which abstractions become possible. Syntactically, the tendency to rely upon co-ordination of main clauses – joined by 'and' or 'then' – continues until about age 10, after which there is a rapid increase in subordinate clauses, particularly relative clauses. Certain grammatical relationships, however, those signalled by 'although', 'unless', or 'if . . . then' for example, are not mastered until about the age 15, if ever. Nor does syntactic development end at 15, for educated adults go on developing and improving their writing performance, sometimes for the rest of their lives. Likewise, of course, the educated adult goes on learning more and more about the universe and so has more and more to write about.

Teaching the ability to read and write is teaching the *use* of English. It is possible, and no doubt desirable, to teach *about* English, but it is not the same thing. Any argument for teaching about English, and about language in general, rests accordingly upon the fact that the phenomenon is important, and directly relevant to human beings, rather than upon any claim for improvement in skill. Perhaps knowing more about language, and particularly one's own language, does improve the ability to use it; perhaps not. What matters is that we should not regard ourselves as properly educated if all we know about language has been acquired by hearsay. Teachers in particular, whatever their subject, have a responsibility to inform themselves about what language is and how it functions, so that they may come to understand how it may and indeed must be used as part of the teaching process. It has been the intention of this book to contribute towards that end.

Additional Reading

Atkinson, P. (1985), *Language, Structure and Reproduction* (London: Methuen).

Barnes, D. (1976), *From Communication to Curriculum* (Harmondsworth: Penguin).

Bellack, A. A. (ed.) (1973), *Studies in the Classroom Language* (New York: Teachers College Press).

Brown, R. (1973), *A First Language: The Early Stages* (London: George Allen & Unwin).

Bullock, A. (1975), *A Language for Life* (London: HMSO).

Cazden, C. B. et al. (eds) (1972), *Functions of Language in the Classroom* (New York: Teachers College Press).

Davies, A. (ed.) (1977), *Language and Learning in Early Childhood* (London: Heinemann Educational).

Department of Education and Science (1982), *Bullock Revisited: a discussion paper by HMI* (London: HMSO).

Department of Education and Science (1988a), *Report of the Committee of Inquiry into the Teaching of English (The Kingman Report)* (London: HMSO).

Department of Education and Science, National Curriculum Council (1988b), *English for Ages 5–11: Proposals of The Secretary of State for Education and The Secretary of State for Wales* (London: DES & Welsh Office).

Department of Education and Science, National Curriculum Council (1989), *English for Ages 5–16: Proposals of The Secretary of State for Education and The Secretary of State for Wales* (London: DES & Welsh Office).

Durkin, K. (1986), *Language Development in the School Years* (Beckenham, Kent: Croom Helm).

Edwards, A. D. and Furlong, V. J. (1978), *The Language of Teaching* (London: Heinemann).

Edwards, V. (1979), *The West Indian Language Issue in British Schools: Challenges and Responses* (London: Routledge & Kegan Paul).

Edwards, V. (1983), *Language in Multicultural Classrooms* (London: Batsford).

Francis, H. (1979), *Language in Teaching and Learning* (London: George Allen & Unwin).

Gilham, B. (1986), *The Language of School Subjects* (London: Heinemann).

Hickman, J. and Kimberley, K. (1988), *Teachers, Language and Learning* (London: Routledge).

Horn, T. (ed.) (1970), *Reading for the Disadvantaged* (New York: Harcourt, Brace & World).

Hunt, K. (1965), *Grammatical Structures Written at Three Grade Levels* (Champaign, Ill.: N.C.T.E.).

Hurt, H. T. et al. (1978), *Communication in the Classroom* (Reading, Mass.: Addison-Wesley).

Kress, G. R. (1982), *Learning to Write* (London: Routledge & Kegan Paul).

Linguistic Minorities Project (1983), *Linguistic Minorities in England* (London: Heinemann Educational).

Linguistic Minorities Project (1985), *Other Languages of England* (London: Routledge & Kegan Paul).

Loban, W. D. (1963), *The Language of Elementary Schoolchildren* (Champaign, Ill.: N.C.T.E.).

Mackay, D., Thompson, B., and Schaub, P. (1978), *Breakthrough to Literacy: Teacher's Manual* (London: Longman for the Schools Council).

Martin, N. et al. (1976), *Writing and Learning Across the Curriculum, 11–16* (Ward Lock Educational for the Schools Council).

Olsson, D. R. et al. (1985), *Literacy, Language and Learning: The Nature and Consequences of Reading and Writing* (Cambridge: CUP).

Painter, C. (1985), *Learning the Mother Tongue* (Oxford: OUP).

Piaget, J. and Inhelder, B. (1977), *The Psychology of the Child* (London: Routledge & Kegan Paul).

Piaget, J. (1977), *The Origin of Intelligence in the Child* (Harmondsworth: Penguin).

Piaget, J. (1978), *The Development of Thought: Equilibration of Cognitive Structures* (Oxford: Blackwell).

Pulaski, M. A. S. (1980), *Understanding Piaget: An Introduction to Children's Cognitive Development*, revised edn (London and New York: Harper Row).

Robertson, I. (1980), *Language Across the Curriculum: Four Case Studies*, Schools Council Working Paper 67 (London: Methuen).

Sinclair, J. M. and Coulthard, R. M. (1975), *Towards an Analysis of Discourse: The English Used by Teachers and Pupils* (Oxford: OUP).

Sinclair, J. M. and Brazil, D. (1982), *Teacher Talk* (Oxford: OUP).

Spolsky, B. (ed.) (1972), *The Language Education of Minority Children* (Rowley, Mass.: Newbury House).

Stubbs, M. (1976), *Language, Schools and Classrooms* (London: Methuen).

Stubbs, M. (1980), *The Sociolinguistics of Reading and Writing* (London: Routledge & Kegan Paul).

Stubbs, M. (1986), *Educational Linguistics* (London: Blackwell).

Sutcliffe, D. (1983), *British Black English* (Oxford: Blackwell).

Thornton, G. (1980), *Teaching Writing: The Development of Written Language Skills* (London: Edward Arnold).

UNESCO (1953), *The Use of Vernacular Languages in Education* (Paris: UNESCO).

Vygotsky, L. S. (1962), *Thought and Language* (Cambridge, Mass.: M.I.T. Press).

Wells, G. (ed.) (1981), *Learning Through Interaction: The Study of Language Development* (Cambridge: CUP).

Wells, G. (ed.) (1985), *Language Development in the Pre-school Years* (Cambridge: CUP).

Wells, G. (1987), *The Meaning Makers: Children Learning Language and Using Language to Learn* (Portsmouth: Heinemann Educational).

Wells, G. (1989), *Language, Learning and Education* (Windsor: N.F.E.R.-Nelson).

Index